CONNEMARA & MAYO
Mountain, Coastal & Island Walks

Paul Phelan worked in research and marketing in Ireland and overseas before starting his own consultancy business. He lives and works in Connemara, enjoys taking people on walks on the hills and islands, and provides guiding services via www.walkconnemara.com.

Lough Inagh and the eastern Bens: Derryclare (left), Bencorr (centre), and Bencorrbeg (right).

CONNEMARA & MAYO

Mountain, Coastal & Island Walks

A Walking Guide

Paul Phelan

The Collins Press

FIRST PUBLISHED IN 2011 BY
The Collins Press
West Link Park
Doughcloyne
Wilton
Cork

Reprinted 2011, 2012, 2013, 2015, 2016, 2017

British Library Cataloguing in Publication Data

Phelan, Paul.
Connemara & Mayo : a walking guide : mountain, coastal
& island walks.

1. Walking—Ireland—Connemara—Guidebooks. 2.
Walking— Ireland—Mayo (County)—Guidebooks. 3.
Connemara

(Ireland)—Guidebooks. 4. Mayo (Ireland : County)—
Guidebooks.

I. Title

796.5'1'094173-dc22

ISBN-13: 9781848891029

Design and typesetting by Fairways Design

Typeset in Avenir

Printed in Poland by Białostockie Zakłady Graficzne SA

Contents

South Mayo 86

North Mayo 122

Acknowledgements

I would like to thank Michael Gibbons for the recommendation, guidance and encouragement. Special thanks to Brigid Sealy for the proofreading, document management and sustained support. I would like to acknowledge being introduced to most of these wonderful walks by the leaders of Na Beanna Beola hillwalking club (particularly Sean O'Farrell, Alacoque O'Sullivan, Eileen Brady, Jamie Thomas and Louis Brennan). Thanks to all the other leaders and walkers who have shared their knowledge and experience of these walks with me. I would also like to acknowledge the learning gained from tutors (particularly Marie Louise Heffernan) and fellow learners on the VTOS Letterfrack Marine and Countryside Guide course.

Photo Credits

All photographs by the author except for: pp. ii/iii, 2/3, 6, 56, 83 and 98/99 by Sean O'Farrell (Sean O'Farrell Photography); pp. 13, 34/35 and 93 by Brigid Sealy.

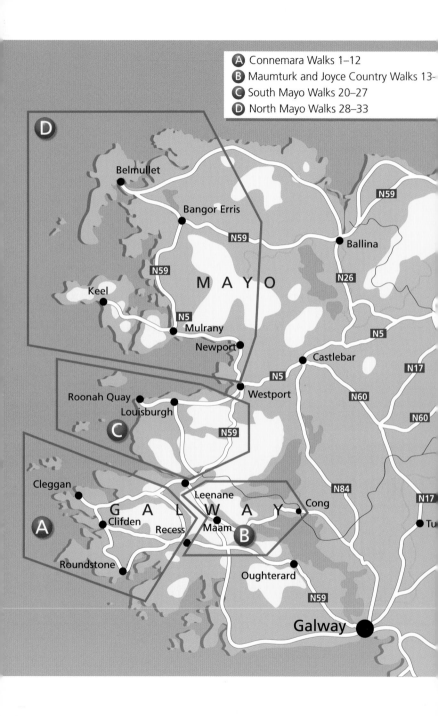

Introduction

This book describes thirty-three of the best coastal, hill and mountain walks in Connemara and Mayo, an area with dramatic scenery combining mountains, valleys, lakes, bogs and sea. This countryside is also distinctive for its wildness, quietness and relatively unspoilt nature. These qualities make it an attractive area to explore, walk and retreat from urban life; but it is a fragile environment which needs to be cared for.

Detailed instructions are provided for each walk. They range from short (about 2 hour) flat walks over surfaced or well-worn paths, through 3- to 4-hour walks on open hillsides or mountains and on to strenuous challenging day-long hikes over rough mountain summits.

The walks are divided into four geographic sections, corresponding to natural groups from different parts of Connemara and Mayo. There are twelve walks in Connemara, seven in The Maumturks/Joyce County, eight in South Mayo and six in North Mayo. A map is provided for each section showing where each of the walks starts. Each section is structured with the easiest walks described first, with the following walks getting progressively more difficult.

It has not been possible to include every interesting walk in Connemara and Mayo; pressure of space, time and access uncertainties has meant that some excellent walks have been left out, e.g. Cashel Hill, Killary Famine Walk, Gleninagh, Maumonght, the Twelve Bens Challenge, Benlevy, Devilsmother, Bunacunneen and Maumtrasna. But these and other walks are suggested as alternatives to similar walks that are included (particularly the easier ones).

This book does not include detailed sections on geology, flora, fauna or other specialities which have been well covered in other publications. However, some specific references are made to these features and other information of interest as they are encountered in particular walks.

Times

An estimate of the time it will take to complete the walk is provided, based on the total distance and ascent. Times for the vast majority of walks are estimated on the basis of 1 minute per 10m of ascent and 3km per hour for walking on open hillside, increasing to 4km per hour for flat surfaced paths. Estimated times for walks that are over 3 hours include a short 5–10 minute stop every 2 hours or so. Therefore you may need to adjust these time estimates depending on your own pace, breaks and the size of your group. For a small number of walks, the steadier pace of 3.5–4km per hour has been assumed in order to meet ferry (Clare Island) or possible daylight constraints (The Glencoaghan Horseshoe).

Walk grades and levels of difficulty

Each walk is graded on a scale of 1 to 5, according to the level of difficulty. None of the walks in this book requires ropes or rock-climbing gear.

Grade	Distance (km)	Total Ascent (m)	Total Time (hours)	Terrain
1. Easy	5.5–9.8	70–250	1.5–3	low-level, surfaced roads, paths, grassy tracks or beach
2. Moderate	7.1–12.1	328–510	2.5–4	some open hillside
3. Difficult	6.7–15.7	470–976	3.5–6	mostly open hillside, some steep rocky exposed mountainous ground
4. Strenuous	11.8–15	960–1,169	5–7	rough, rocky, mountainous, exposed steep ground with some light scrambling
5 Challenging	14.3–24.3	1,660–2,340	6–14	steady pace, very rough exposed mountains, with significant steep rocky ground, and scrambling

Safety

Climbing hills and mountains can be a demanding and sometimes dangerous activity. Steep ground, exposed rock and cliffs – which are a feature of many of the walks in this book – bring a serious risk of injury from a slip or a fall. In addition, there are other risks: strong winds or misty conditions can develop; loose rocks can fall and hit a person below; hypothermia can set in; underlying health conditions can be triggered by strenuous exercise. While this book highlights some particular dangers, it is not possible to list them all. Therefore, all readers are warned to take reasonable precautions before setting out. In particular, it is recommended that walkers have a proper map and compass to navigate effectively in poor visibility and know the

weather forecast. Walkers should also ensure they have sufficient physical fitness and experience before taking on any of these hill or mountain walks.

Ticks

Ticks are common in the moorland and grasslands of Connemara and Mayo. A small proportion are infected with bacteria that can lead to Lyme disease in humans. Check yourself as soon as possible after a walk and remove any ticks using a small tweezers (take care to remove the complete tick including the head and mouth). Early symptoms of Lyme disease include a reddish rash possibly with flu-like symptoms; consult your doctor if you notice these after being bitten.

Access

The walks described do not represent a right of way; you access land at the discretion of the landowner. While there are currently no major issues accessing the walks in this book, if you meet a landowner it is recommended that you ask for permission to cross their land; if permission is refused, you should accept the landowner's position and leave immediately. Access to land for walkers has the potential to become a contentious issue, so respect for landowners is important for continued access..

You should also respect landowners' property and be particularly careful with parking, gates and fences. Avoid farm animals and crops. Never block entrances to roads, paths, tracks or gates; take particular care to park cars so that large vehicles (tractors and even trucks) will not be impeded. Always close gates – unless it is clear that a landowner has deliberately left them open. When crossing gates or fences, try to minimise the impact; climb gates on the hinged side (rather than the end that opens); cross fences at a point where it is easy to cross; groups should cross a fence sequentially at one point; after you have crossed a fence re-fix it as you found it (or better). Dogs are not generally welcome because wildlife and sheep can get very stressed by their presence.

The access situation is subject to change. Walks which are currently accessible may become less so. An update on access issues will be posted on www.walkconnemara.com. Your comments on access issues or experiences would be welcome by email to walkconnemara@gmail.com.

Leave no Trace

There has been an awareness of the fragile nature of the environment and heritage of the Connemara and Mayo area. You are encouraged to follow the principles of 'Leave No Trace', an ethics programme designed to promote responsible outdoor recreation. The basic idea is to make it hard for others to see or hear you and to literally leave no trace of your visit. This can be expanded into the seven principles (see www.leavenotraceireland.org for details):

1. Plan ahead and prepare
2. Be considerate of others
3. Respect farm animals and wildlife
4. Travel and camp on durable ground
5. Leave what you find
6. Dispose of waste properly
7. Minimise the effects of fire

CONNEMARA

This section is the largest in this book, with twelve walks, covering all levels of difficulty. There is an easy coastal walk (1, Omey), a gentle island walk (2, Inishbofin) and a variety of hill walks, including the paved path to the exposed top of Diamond Hill in the Connemara National Park (Walk 3). On the very strenuous end of the scale there are the Glencorbet and Glencoaghan Horseshoes (Walks 11 & 12). In between there is a good range of mountain walks, from moderate to difficult, several of which feature fine sea views (e.g. 7, Tully Mountain; 8, Benchoona; and 9, Doughruagh and Lemnaheltia).

The coastal landscape of Connemara (Conmaicne mara: the descendants of Conmac by the sea) features beautiful beaches, sand dunes and rocky peninsulas surrounding sheltered bays. The mountainous areas feature bare rocky summits – many of quartzite – surrounded by blanket bog. Connemara's geology is actually very diverse.

The Twelve Bens and the Northern Bens (Doughruagh, Garraun and Benchoona) represent one of Ireland's most important conservation sites. This mountainous area includes a wide variety of habitats, eight of which are listed in the EU Habitats Directive. Extensive active blanket bog – along with alpine heath, machair and oak forest – designate it a Special Area of Conservation. Rare species which support this designation include the freshwater pearl mussel, Atlantic salmon, the otter and the plant Slender Naiad. Sphagnum moss is widespread throughout the lowland.

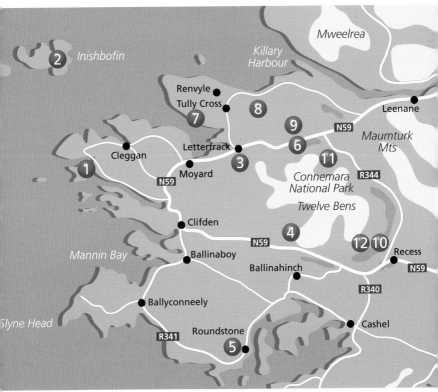

Connemara Walks 1–12

1. OMEY ISLAND

Introduction: This is an easy walk around the small tidal island of Omey (*Iomaí*: bed of St Feichín). It is accessible on foot except for about three hours either side of full tide (i.e. about six hours in total). The walk features fine views of the sea and the surrounding islands, ancient archaeological sites and rare machair/sand dune habitats. Omey Strand can be quite wet, but the walk is suited to walking sandals (or bare feet for much of it).

Grade: I Easy *Time:* 2.5 hours *Distance:* 7.9km *Ascent:* I10m
Maps: OS *Discovery 37*, Tim Robinson's *Connemara Part 2*

Start/finish: L578564 car park beside the slipway (just south of Claddaghduff Quay on OS). This is at the end of the small road beside the church (and just opposite the school) at Claddaghduff (8km west of the N59 junction 2.5km north of Clifden).

Route Description: Head west across the sand towards the rocks in the middle of the wide strand that joins the island to the mainland. Continue towards a house prominent on a headland on the right of the island, keeping the sea water on your right. This is a special spot for sea birds. On your left you can see the Omey graveyard (*Ula Bhreandáin*: St Brendan's Altar) which is in use today; the sight of a funeral crossing the beach is quite spiritual.

As the water edge brings you closer to the island, take the sandy path that follows the fence above the rocks. Continue along a small beach, cross the stream at the far end and climb up the small hill, which is an ancient midden site (burrowing rabbits often bring up ancient debris). The hill reveals a larger beach, the right-hand side of which is a good place to swim. As you walk across the beach, notice the pier of Aughrus (Tonashindilla on the map) to the northwest. About halfway across the beach the fence on your left turns away from the sand. Follow this up onto the grass and enter a little hollow. Here are the roofless remains of *Teampaill Feichín*, the medieval parish church of Omey, on the site of St Feichín's original abbey (he also founded abbeys in nearby High Island and Cong).

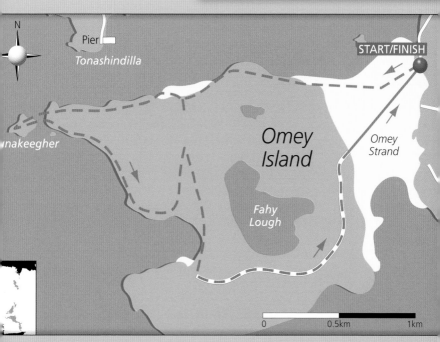

Omey Tidal Island Walk

N

Pier

Tonashindilla

START/FINISH

nakeegher

Omey
Island

Omey
Strand

Fahy
Lough

0   0.5km   1km

*Remains of chapel on nearby High Island. The walls have small alcoves,
which provided shelter for the monks.*

Return to the beach and continue left along the sandy path that goes below a small dune ridge on your left, with distinctive big red and brown rocks that have fallen off the top. At the end of this ridge, in the eroding grass and sand, is an ancient graveyard, from which human remains often protrude.

Continue along the beach and over grassy hillocks beside the rocky shore to the rougher northwesterly end of Omey (*Béal an Oileáin:* Mouth of the Island). Provided the tide is out and conditions are not stormy, you can go out to the small grassy island (Illaunakeegher on the OS map) for a fine perspective.

Return to the main island and follow its shoreline to the right and southeast past a stony beach (*Trá na nÉan:* Beach of the Birds). The waves can be impressive along this stretch as you pick up a grassy track following the rocky coast south (there are shell middens up to the east). Notice the uninhabited Cruagh Island to the west, and further north, High Island, which has impressive remains of the monastic site founded by St Feichín. In stormy weather, monks would wait here in Omey before moving to High Island when the weather permitted. Follow the coast as it turns to the east into a bay with a stony beach, passing the beautiful holy well (*Tobar Feichín*) with a good number of talisman or amulet objects (to bring good luck or protection to its owner or a deceased loved one).

To visit the beautiful sand hills, from the holy well head back north towards the hill marking the highest point of Omey. These sand dunes form part of Omey's rare machair habitat. Return south to the stony beach east of the holy well; go down to the water's edge to view the 'underwater' turf – evidence of the rising sea levels since the bog was formed. At the far end of the beach, climb up the grassy slope – past the shell midden in the sandy cliff face – to the road. The island's only permanent resident lives here.

Take the road left, passing Fahy Lough (there has been a recent report of a monster sighting here). Continue along the road, past several houses and a sad old ruin. Notice the lovely views of the mainland beaches of Fountainhill as you make your way back to Omey Strand at the other side of the island. Cross the beach to return to the car park; people still dig for shellfish here.

Alternatives and Variations: Drive over to the island and park near the graveyard to shorten the walk by 30 minutes. Alternatively, the walk can be extended at the end of the island road. When you reach the beach, go to the right towards the rocks directly east, which provide for good swimming once the tide comes in. Returning from this shore to the car park will add about 15 minutes to the walk. A longer detour – adding about 1 hour – is to continue to the south over the rocks of the Fountainhill shore. This leads to a string of beautiful beaches, the first of which has a small track (beside the stream) leading back to a road. Take the road to the right (not left!) and then left onto the main road. Then take the next left back to the beach just below the car park.

The tidal island of Finish 4km south of Carna (L778319) is a similar walk to Omey, but access requires a spring (low) tide.

St Feichín's Holy Well (top) and view west from it (bottom)

2. INISHBOFIN

Introduction: This is a short, low-level, moderate-grade walk around Inishbofin – a beautiful island with great walking potential. There are super views of the sea, the surrounding islands and the mainland mountains. This walk is based around a day trip on the regular ferry service from Cleggan. It focuses on Knock, the southeast corner of the island; there are two or three other similar walks on Inishbofin. This walk features some rare machair and sand dune habitats. Much of the island is a Special Area of Conservation (designated for corncrakes and seals), with large numbers of wintering barnacle geese. To safely visit the castle, you need to know the tide times. Near the village where you get the ferry, there are several megalithic tombs (Cleggan Farm, Sellerna and Sheeauns) and standing stones (Cloon, Sheeauns, Ballynew). The tidal Omey island walk is also nearby.

Grade: 2 Moderate **Time:** 3.5 hours **Distance:** 8.4km **Ascent:** 328m
Maps: OS *Discovery 37*, Tim Robinson's *Connemara Part 2*, Inishbofin
Development Company's *Map of Inishbofin Island*

Start/finish: L537648, at the main pier on Inishbofin. Currently there is a ferry departure from the pier (quay in OS map) in Cleggan (L602584) every day at 11.30 a.m., returning from Inishbofin at 5 p.m.; the walk below is based around this schedule (see www. inishbofinislanddiscovery.com). There is usually room to park near the Cleggan pier, but in summer or busy weekends you may have to pay for private parking nearby. When the ferry leaves the quay in Cleggan, look across the bay for a portal tomb perched on the opposite shoreline. As the ferry turns into the mouth of Inishbofin's harbour, you get an impressive view of Cromwell's Barracks perched on the right overlooking the harbour.

Safety: High winds will make this walk dangerous, particularly near the cliffs. To safely cross to Cromwell's Barracks you need the tide to be less than halfway in.

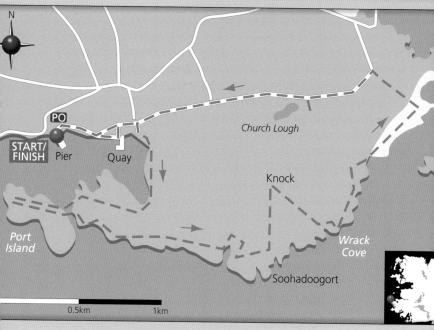

Inishbofin, Knock and Southeast Coastal Walk

N

PO

START/FINISH Pier

Quay

Church Lough

Knock

Port Island

Wrack Cove

Soohadoogort

0.5km   1km

View of Croagh Patrick from the east end of Inishbofin

Route Description: At the end of the pier, turn right and walk along the road, past the church (ignore the road going up left) and continue to the corner at Day's Bar. (If the tide is low, you can go straight down and walk the rocky shore in front of the hotel to the small road 150m away). Head left up the steep hill, turn right at the top and then take the next small road right down to the shore. Take the track left and through the gate – past the remains of a limekiln – onto the grassy hillside overlooking the inner Bofin Harbour with its small island (*Glasoileán*, with ruins of a curing station). This strategic natural harbour is very sheltered. Continue south beside the shore and alongside a wall with a low gate; go through carefully. Head westwards across the grass towards the castle; keep right of a hill and go down to the beach. Continue along the beach towards the castle: provided the tide is out, cross over to Port Island and visit Cromwell's Barracks (bear in mind that the crossing will not be safe approaching a full tide). This is the remains of a Cromwellian fort, with diamond-shaped bastions at its four corners and an impressive arched entrance. The barracks were built in the seventeenth century. Cromwell's forces used the fort as a prison for Catholic clergy and to thwart pirates.

Return from Port Island and climb the small grassy hill to the right following the creek (*Béal na Brád*) out towards the sea. Turn east and go alongside the shore past lake Loughnabraud (*Loch na Brád*) to cross the fence. Continue along the grassy coastline past small coves to the dramatic narrow creek *Uaimh na bhFiach*.

Continue along the Ooghdoty (OS map) shoreline to another small cove at Soohadoogort (*Scoth Dúghort*), before turning north to climb the hill (Knock 81m), your highest point on this walk. Enjoy the view back over the middle and west of the island. Descend southeastwards back to the coastline at the broad and stunning Wreck Cove; it is said that Cromwell's forces landed here after their ship was fired on entering the harbour.

Follow the coast northwest before continuing inside a stone wall (keeping it on your right) and crossing a gate to go down to the spectacular Dumhach beach. Notice the island of Inishlyon to the east (connected to the beach at low tide via slippery rocks), which has a very old cooking site (*fulacht fiadh*). Walk halfway along the fine sands with tiny cowrie shells and take the track beyond the grass (a rare machair habitat) through a gate to the road. Turn left and walk up to the walled St Colman's cemetery, with the remains of a thirteenth-century chapel. St Colman founded the original monastery here in the

The beautiful narrow creek of Uaimh na bhFiach

seventh century, after leaving Lindisfarne following the rejection of the Celtic way of calculating Easter at the Synod of Whitby. The holy well to the southwest is associated with St Flannan.

Return to the road and go left, passing the Inishbofin Hostel and the Dolphin Hotel on your right. Continue west past the large hotel on your left and down to the harbour beside the new St Colman's church. Turn right to go to the pier (left brings you back to the pub). The community centre behind the shop has basic refreshments, information on the island and public toilets.

3. DIAMOND HILL

Introduction: This is a short, moderate-grade walk over a trail with a short, steep climb to a rocky summit. The trail includes paths, boardwalks, and paving built while the mountain was temporarily closed due to severe erosion from large numbers of walkers. Situated beside the former Quaker village of Letterfrack, in the Connemara National Park, between the Twelve Bens and the coast, there are fine views. Diamond Hill (Bengooria or *Binn Ghuaire*) gets its name from the glittering quartzite top, which glistens in the sun – particularly after rain.

Grade: 2 Moderate **Time:** 2.5 hours **Distance:** 7km **Ascent:** 510m
Maps: OS *Discovery 37*

Start/finish: L711573 at the car park entrance (free, open all year round) of the Connemara National Park, which is accessed from the N59 just west of Letterfrack.

Route Description: Enter the park and go down to the left of the visitor centre and take the (Sruffaunboy) path marked 'Diamond Hill' past the playground. Go through the (deer) gates and follow the gravel path to until you take the left 'Lower Diamond Walk' up steps near a stream and up along the bog boardwalk to a large boulder. Go left here onto the 'Upper Diamond Hill Walk' for 0.5km to the point where the trail splits, and take the left route to the summit. A legend says that Fionn MacCumhaill's dog Bran chased a large stag from the side of Diamond Hill to Lemnaheltia (*Léim na hEilte*: Leap of the Stag) where the hound fell off a cliff.

At the summit you can see fine views of the sea, the Bens and Kylemore Abbey. Continue along the narrow summit to the cairn. Descend by passing the cairn and following the trail down the steep-stepped far side of the mountain; care is required here. The trail returns along a lovely valley to join the path you came up. Take this all the way back to the visitor centre (or to extend your walk by 10 minutes, go left at the large boulder and return to the car park along the 'Bog Road').

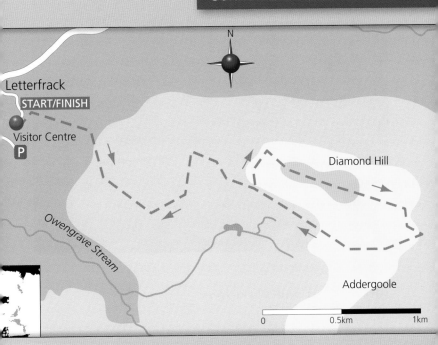

Diamond Hill Walk from the Connemara National Park

N

Letterfrack
START/FINISH
Visitor Centre
P

Diamond Hill

Owengrave Stream

Addergoole

0   0.5km   1km

Approach to Diamond Hill, showing boardwalk and paved path

Alternatives and Variations: To experience what is a very lively locale – adding only about 10 minutes' walking time – park in the village of Letterfrack, walk through the Connemara West centre (the former Letterfrack Industrial School, now a Furniture College and community development campus) via the gap in the low stone wall leading to a tarmac path. Pass the line of buildings (crèche, Radio, Ellis Hall) on the left and go up the steps between the cottages in front of you (rear of the main building). Pass the church and up more steps, turning right into the small road. Pass the old Monastery Hostel and enter the National Park. At the visitor centre, take the left path past the children's playground and up through the gates. On completing the Diamond return to the visitor centre (the Park includes several gentle nature trails such as the Ellis Wood), and exit via the gate you entered. On the way down to the village take a look at the hostel, Letterfrack Industrial School Graveyard and the Furniture College (main building below church). Similar alternatives to Diamond Hill include Cashel Hill (L800437) and Benlevy (M105549).

Looking west from the Diamond towards Tully Mountain, with Ballynakill Bay, and Inishbofin (left horizon) and the edge of Inishturk (right horizon). The stone path of the Diamond Walk is just visible in the foreground.

View of the Twelve Bens from the east side of the Diamond

4. BENGLENISKY, BENGOWER AND BENLETTERY

Introduction: A short, difficult-grade mountain walk taking in three adjacent peaks in the Twelve Bens. The walk described requires two cars, but can be extended into a loop requiring just one car. A longer extension includes several additional Bens – potentially going right around the challenging Owenglin Horseshoe.

Grade: 3 Difficult **Time:** 3.5 hours **Distance:** 6.7km **Ascent:** 635m
Maps: OS *Discovery 37, 44* (for the Benlettery section), Harvey's *Connemara* (useful for some details not marked on OS map)

Start: Leave one car in front of the Benlettery Youth Hostel (L777482) and drive west along the N59 for 2.5km to the junction (L751487) on the right (just after a small church also on the right). Take this small road right (north) for 2km up to the top of the hill where the broad entrance to a recently cut forest on the right provides parking for several cars at L750501.

Finish: L777482 at Benlettery Youth Hostel.

Route Description: From the entrance to the former forest, walk north on the road for 200m past the remains of the forestry, turning right (east) to cross the wet ditch and follow the fence up over the wet bog towards the mountain. Continue east up the drier and steepening hillside as it undulates and gets rockier. To the northwest you will notice a quarry at *Barr na nÓrán*; this is where the distinctive green Connemara marble is extracted. The climb to the top is steep but short; continue east, past rock outcrops and several small cairns, before reaching the summit of Benglenisky (*Binn Ghleann Uisce*: Peak of the Valley of Water, 516m, with cairn). There are fine views of the six additional Bens that make up the Owenglin Horseshoe, the lakes of Roundstone bog to the south and Clifden to the west.

From Benglenisky, continue east over the rocky top past a boggy hollow (below 506m on Harvey's) to the broad bog plateau. Climb gently a little north of east to pass a cairn on your right above a small cliff (560m on Harvey's). At this cairn turn left a little to take a

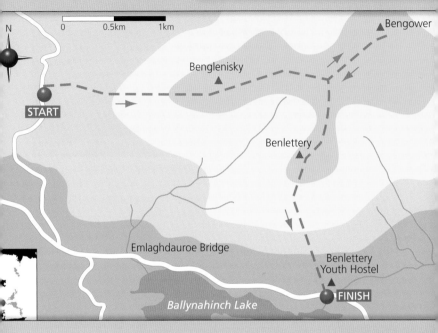

N

0   0.5km   1km

Bengower

Benglenisky

START

Benlettery

Emlaghdauroe Bridge

Benlettery
Youth Hostel

FINISH

Ballynahinch Lake

*Owenglin Horseshoe viewed from Benglenisky with (l–r): Muckanaght,
Benfree, Benbaun and Benbreen*

Approaching Bengower (centre) from Benglenisky with Benbreen (left)

northeasterly direction along a flat area from which a faint track climbs gently; the track gets clearer as the ground steepens, taking you up through a rocky gap, past a boggy area to the exposed summit of Bengower (*Binn Gabhar*: Peak of the Goat, 664m, erroneously marked as 'Glengower' on the OS map). There is a cairn perched above the cliffs falling off into the Glencoaghan valley.

From Bengower, retrace your steps back southwest along the track to the cairn you passed between the three mountains (560m on Harvey's). At the cairn, turn left a little, and descend in a southerly direction to a saddle. Then climb south up a short ridge that bends right (southwest) to the rock-strewn top leading to the summit of Benlettery (*Binn Leitrí*: Peak of the Wet Hillsides) or Bendouglas (*Binn Dúghlais*: Peak of the Black Stream, 577m with cairn). View the spectacular vista of lakes, bog, hills and sea, as the late Joss Lynam described it: 'the fantastic land and water jigsaw of South Connemara'.

The descent from Benlettery needs care, as there are crags to be avoided and a small area of steep ground to be negotiated. First head down the spur to the south, through the rocky outcrops. Then follow the spur to the southwest along the well-worn tracks between some crags and cliffs; be prepared to use your hands at one or two steep spots. Below the rocks, take the eroded bog track that leads south-southeast down the heathery moorland towards the Youth Hostel. Cross a fence and go through the remains of an old village before keeping right of the Hostel to cross the fence to the front garden and then out to the road where your other car has (hopefully) been parked.

Alternatives and Variations: The walk described can be approached in reverse. If you have only one car, there are two options: extend into a loop by walking back along the N59; if you want to avoid this 4km road walk, leave the car at L758486 near the Emlaghdauroe Bridge, enabling you to follow the beautiful river up to the north, cover the three peaks and return via the spur descending west from halfway down Benlettery. There are several extension options from Bengower including the complete Owenglin Horseshoe option: carefully begin the northerly descent of Bengower about 100m west of the summit, preparing for the essential use of hands for the steep but firm rocky stage (not for the faint-hearted!); from the saddle below, climb Benbreen on the left-hand side of the scree; from Benbreen continue north and then northeast down to Maumina; exit west along the stream to the forest road and back to the start or continue to Benbaun, Benfree, Muckanaght and the saddle west of Bencullagh before descending south along the stream to the road – turning right to return over the bridge past *Barr na nÓrán* to the start (a challenging 9–11 hour hike in all).

Benlettery from halfway down Bengower

5. ERRISBEG

Introduction: This is an introductory, difficult-grade, looped hill walk. It involves just one short but stiff climb and descent over open ground followed by flat road, beach and grass terrain. The hill features rare heathers along with fine views of the sea and the surrounding islands. The walk includes the spectacular beaches of the peninsula that gives Errisbeg its name (*Iorras Beag*: small peninsula), featuring rare machair and sand dune habitats. By excluding the beaches, it is possible to shorten the walk to 4 hours (by walking back along the main road), or to 2.5–3 hours (with a car drop or taxi pick-up).

To drive the spectacular 'Bog Road' (through Roundstone Bog, with its multitude of small lakes), go north out of Roundstone on the R341 for about 5km and take the small road left at a dangerous right-hand bend in the main road. Alternatively, the opposite part of the R341 goes past the beautiful Ballyconneeley Bay, the superb small 'coral' (actually calcified seaweed) beaches of Mannin Bay, the site of Marconi's first transatlantic wireless communication, and the landing place of the first transatlantic flight by Alcock and Brown (in 1919). MacDara's Island, in South Connemara, with its spectacular church, can be reached from the quay at Mace (L741316).

Grade: 3 Difficult **Time:** 5 hours **Distance:** 15.4km **Ascent:** 470m
Maps: OS *Discovery 44*

Start/finish: L724400, in the picturesque village of Roundstone; there is parking opposite the Roundstone House Hotel.

Safety: Do not attempt this walk in very windy weather and be prepared for mist.

Route Description: From the car park, walk north down the hill and take the narrow road up left at O'Dowd's Bar. Keep straight on this road – through a crossroads – and up to where it ends at a small house with a beautiful ruin in the garden. Go through the small wooden gate beyond and to the left of this house, and follow the track up onto the open hillside.

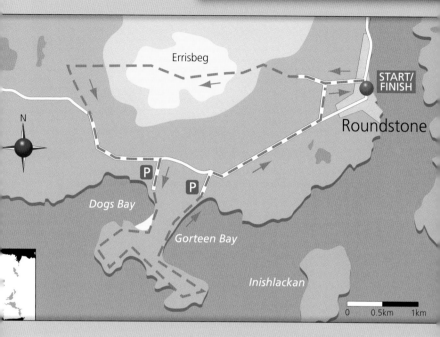

Errisbeg Looped Walk including beaches

Errisbeg

START/ FINISH

Roundstone

N

P

P

Dogs Bay

Gorteen Bay

Inishlackan

0   0.5km   1km

View south from the top of Errisbeg, over the beaches of Dogs Bay (right) and Gorteen (left)

View from Errisbeg to the southeast over Inishlackan and the bays of Roundstone and Bertraghboy with MacDara's Island just visible beyond the distant headland

Continue on the track in a westerly direction, climbing the bog and increasingly rocky hill of Errisbeg East (*Iorras Beag Thoir,* 252m). This habitat supports a very wide range of mountain heathers, including rare ones more typical of the Iberian peninsula. As you reach the cairn, notice the panoramic view to the east over the bays of Roundstone and Bertraghboy, including MacDara's Island (the sixth-century hermitage of the patron saint of Connemara's fishermen) and the Twelve Bens to the north.

From this subsidiary summit, descend in a westerly direction to a small saddle, and climb the rocky top of Errisbeg itself (300m, with concrete pillar), which has fine views of the beaches to the south.

Descend carefully in a westerly direction, avoiding some steep rocks, and picking up a grassy gully between two cliffs. Keep to the higher ground on the right as you descend carefully towards the bog road in front of Lough Trosca.

You will come down onto a grassy area with clumps of gorse and bell heather. Go right/anticlockwise around a small lake and cross the small stream, turning left when you reach the bog track. Go through the gate and turn left onto the main R341 road. Taking care for cars, continue on the main road for 1.5km and around a bend. Turn right at the sign for Dogs Bay (*Cuan an Mhada*) and walk across the beautiful rare sand made almost completely of the shells of foraminifera, a

Errisbeg East (right, with cairn), with Roundstone Bog and the Twelve Bens in the background

single-celled organism. Continue past the sand dunes to the far end of the beach. Take the track right up to the gate and onto the machair grass, which is an important and protected habitat that is being conserved though a community effort. Pass another beautiful small beach and walk left around Earawalla Point and through a gate to the beach and along the coast (past middens, OS map) to Gorteen Point. Follow the coastline northwest through a gate to Gorteen Beach (*Trá na Feadóige*: Beach of the Plovers) and to the road. Continue up the small road and turn right when you reach the main road R341. Follow this carefully for 2km until you see a small road on your left, marked Errisbeg House. Take this small quiet road for 500m to the crossroads and turn right. This brings you back to the village where you turn right to return to the car park.

Alternatives and Variations: This walk can easily be shortened by 1 hour by continuing along the main R341 road to the starting point instead of turning right to go to the Dogs Bay and Gorteen beaches. The walk can be further shortened to a 2.5–3 hour linear walk by organising transport at the gate onto the R341 (L684397) after descending Errisbeg. Similar alternatives to Errisbeg include nearby Cashel Hill (L800437) with a spectacular wedge tomb to the southwest and Benlevy (M105549) in Joyce Country.

6. MWEELIN

Introduction: This is an introductory, difficult-grade, looped mountain walk with just one hard climb. The walk passes important archaeological sites at the start before going through the Connemara National Park.

Grade: 3 Difficult **Time:** 4 hours **Distance:** 8.4km **Ascent:** 670m
Maps: OS *Discovery 37*

Start/finish: L742582 beside an old stone warehouse on the small road just south of the N59, about 0.4km west of Kylemore Abbey and 1.2km east of Tullywee Bridge (3.5km from Letterfrack). Park carefully beside/opposite the old stone warehouse and don't block the road, which is used by residents and large vehicles.

Route Description: Carefully walk along the very busy main N59 road past Kylemore Abbey. Continue past the abbey's exit for 0.4km, taking great care on the dangerous corner, to the gate on the right. Open the gate and go along the wet tree-lined track. Follow this track over the stream and past the excellent remains of a limekiln; this was used to extract fertiliser from limestone. Continue up the quarry and past the remains of a megalithic (court) tomb to the holy well; there is a children's burial ground just to the south which may have earlier been a monastic site. Continue in a southeasterly direction, until you reach the National Park's deer fence on your right (inaccurately positioned on the OS map). Follow the fence uphill until it turns sharply right. Leave the fence and continue straight uphill into a grassy bowl. Then turn right a little and climb directly – and steeply – up to the summit of Benbaun (477m – not to be confused with the Benbaun that is the highest and in the middle of the Twelve Bens, further south).

Descend in a southerly direction to the saddle before climbing south to reach Benbrack (*Binn Bhreac*, 582m). Turn right and pass the lake before descending in a northwesterly direction along the spur to cross the National Park fence. Watch out for wild goats in this

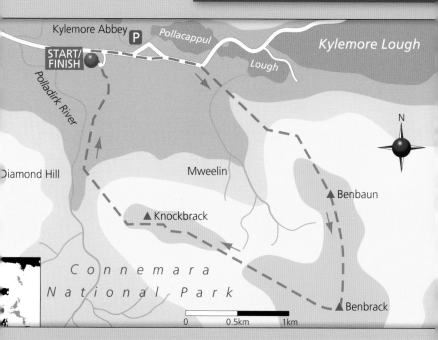

area, but don't approach them. Continue in a more westerly direction, climbing a little to Knockbrack (442m).

From Knockbrack, descend carefully to the west for about 300m, until the slope eases. Then turn a little to the right, taking a northwesterly direction to descend to the banks of the Polladirk River. Continue north beside the river and cross the stile, following the path to the old Kylemore Abbey farm. Take the road to the left, past a house, to the old stone warehouse by the main road.

Alternatives and Variations: This walk can be extended to a long, tough trek (about 7 hours) around the Bens surrounding the Polladirk River valley. This involves heading south to Maumnascalpa, and Muckanaght (taking care with what is a very steep climb, with the final approach to the summit best tackled from the northwest side), and then west to Bencullagh and Maumonght before descending to the Polladirk River and following it to the north to eventually reach the stile leading to the farm (as above).

Wild goats in Connemara National Park

Holy well at Mweelin, with a snow-covered Benbaun and Benbrack in the distance

Main summit cairn of Benbrack with the Maumturks in the distance

7. TULLY MOUNTAIN

Introduction: This is an introductory, difficult-grade, circular mountain walk, the first third of which is along a quiet, small road. It features beautiful sea and mountain views along with several interesting old turf-drying structures and rare birds. Local legend suggests this hill was the scene of an initiation ceremony for new chiefs (from nearby Derryherbert or *Doire na hOirbirt*: Hill of Sacrifice). There is a large number of important archaeological sites on the Renvyle Peninsula: megalithic tombs (Cloonlooaun, Tonadooravaun, Ardnagreevagh), middens (Rusheenduff), a stone row (Derryinver), and promontory forts (Knocknasheeoge, Mullaghglass).

Grade: 3 Difficult **Time:** 4.5 hours **Distance:** 10.6km **Ascent:** 630m **Maps:** OS *Discovery 37*

Start/finish: Derryinver pier or 'Quay' (as marked in OS map) at L688598. There is room to park several cars without impeding this surprisingly busy pier.

Route Description: From the pier, head west along the narrow road for about 3.5km, passing through the small villages of Ardagh and Letter More (where there is a right of way from the road on to the mountain side) until you reach the last house at Letter Beg. Take the grassy road above the house through the gate. Pass between two sheds and through a gate on the right leading up towards another gate visible in the wall further above. Keep the wall on your left – passing a cliff on your left – for about 1.5km to the end of the peninsula. Keep an eye out for small diving and swooping crow-like birds with a sharp 'chaaow' call; they may be rare choughs that nest on ledges in crevices and caves of coastal cliffs.

On the way you will notice Freaghillaun (*Fraochoileán:* Island of the Heather), in the middle of the bay, where it is said that German submarines got fresh water during the Second World War, and *Bráidoileán* (Neck Island) nearer the mainland. Also nearby is the *Scailp Nora Ní Allurain* cave, in which a local O'Halloran man hid after

Tully Mountain Walk from Derryinver Pier

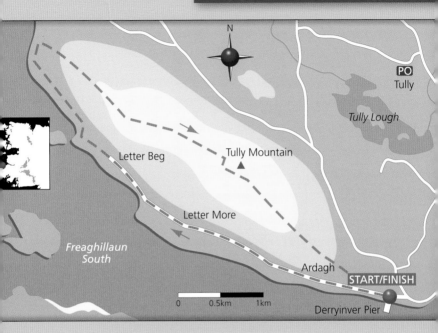

View of the side of Tully Mountain and the sea (including Inishbofin to the left) as seen during first part of this walk.

attacking a landlord in Inishbofin, according to Tim Robinson. Continue along above the beautiful cliffs and coves and watch out for fulmars and shags (cormorant-like birds but smaller)

When the wall starts to rise to meet the cliffs and the spur in front of you, turn right (southeast) to make your way along this large spur towards the first peak of the spine of the mountain (272m).

Once you can see the first peak of the spine 1–1.5km in the distance keep to the valleys just below (i.e. southwest of) the spine to notice several unusual stone-wall structures of about 5–10m in length with a smaller length of wall on one side. These are the remains of 'turf stacks' that were used to dry turf (up to quite recently in this case). After you reach the first peak, look back at the coastal views before passing the lake (Lough Awauma) and heading east for the second of four peaks (306m). This peak has a small cairn 200m further to the east, but you can save energy by staying just south of it.

Next head southeast, through rough heather, to pick up a rough track rising to the (335m) sub-peak of the summit. Tully Mountain itself (356m, with trig point, also known as Letter Hill) is 400m further southeast with the cairn (and fine views of Mweelrea and the Bens).

From the summit, follow the track continuing southeast and pick up the broad southeast spur pointing towards the pier where your car is. Make your way down to the road before the final hill or continue to the gate that leads to a gravel road. On the road take a left to get back to the pier.

View of Tully Mountain from Ross Beach on the other side of Ballynakill Harbour

Turf stack, formerly used to dry the peat used for fuel, overlooking Ballynakill Harbour (including Freaghillaun and Ross Beach) located towards the end of the peninsula approaching the first sub-peak of the Tully Mountain spine.

Alternatives and Variations: Straight up and down from the gate below the summit on the road from Derryinver towards Cashleen to the north; this is very straightforward – about 4km over bog ascending 350m and requiring about 2 hours.

8. BENCHOONA HORSESHOE

Introduction: This is a difficult-grade mountain walk over bog, rock and grass. It features spectacular coastal and mountain views along with conglomerate geology and rare birds (choughs). The beach near the start/finish point is safe for bathing, while the stunning Glassillaun strand is 2km further east.

Grade: 3 Difficult **Time:** 4.5 hours **Distance:** 9.5km **Ascent:** 730m
Maps: OS *Discovery 37*

Start/finish: Lettergesh Beach public car park (L737630, marked 'Carrickglass' on the OS map), at the end of a lane 4.5km east from Tully Cross and 1.2km west of Lettergesh Post Office. The lane is near a bridge with a sign for 'Lettergesh Beach Angling'; take care as you drive beside the stream.

Route Description: Walk back up to the main road and turn left. After 200m (just before a small bridge) go right up the minor road (with *'Cluain Ard'* signs) between two houses (one of which is a B&B). Go through the gate on the right (usually open, with another *'Cluain Ard'* sign), up the lane past another house on the right and through a newer gate (usually closed). Go up this new gravel road beside the stream to the new local water supply system. Take the grassy track on the left leading up beside the rocky stream and fence on your right. Continue past the old concrete bridge – keeping the stream gorge and fence on your right.

Follow the sheep path that contours along the low, but at times, steep-sided valley overlooking the winding stream, keeping above the waterfall until you reach a flat open area with a track leading across to a major tributary coming from the right. Cross the stream here and climb up the steep valley side and follow this tributary. Then head across the open bog towards the spur on the right leading to the jagged northwest ridge of Altnagaighera (Ravine of the Sheep or *Binn Fhraoigh*: Heather Peak). Follow the valley up, keeping to the right of – and just below – the conglomerate outcrops, before climbing the

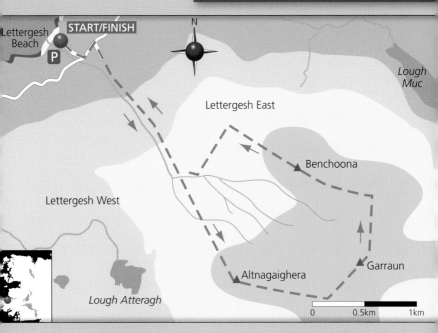

Benchoona Horseshoe from Lettergesh Beach

START/FINISH

Lettergesh Beach

P

N

Lough Muc

Lettergesh East

Benchoona

Lettergesh West

Altnagaighera

Garraun

Lough Atteragh

0   0.5km   1km

steep grassy slopes to the summit (543m, without cairn or marker). Conglomerate rocks feature stones held together in a cement-like base rock. Watch out for the unusual scree (small loose stones) of rounded stones created by the weathering of the conglomerate rock around the summit.

Keep your ears peeled for choughs (pronounced 'chuff') – birds nesting or diving and swooping around some crags or cliffs. These rare and elegant members of the crow family are a little smaller than a rook and are distinguished by a bright red, slightly curved bill, red legs/feet and loud ringing 'chaaow' call.

Continue east past the lake (Loughan) and some small hills, along a broad boggy ridge to a rounded top (556m). Then descend to a boggy saddle before climbing northeastwards over bog, stone and grass past outcrops to Garraun (598m, known locally as *Maolchnoic*: Bald or Rounded Hill), with its summit cairn and spectacular views.

Descend to the north to cross a gap past small lakes, lovely rocky outcrops and small cairns. After crossing between two adjacent lakes, turn left (west-northwest). Keep left of the larger lake (Lough Benchoona, a nice place for lunch) to reach the plateau summit of Benchoona (*Binn Chuanna*, 581m, with two cairns), taking care amongst the maze of outcrops.

Make your final descent via the steep broad spur to the northwest, keeping a little right to avoid crags, to a gap. Follow the boggy spur with outcrops and descend a little before turning left and heading

Benchoona and part of the horseshoe towards Altnagaighera (beyond right view), while Garraun is to the right and behind the main peak.

Upper part of stream leading to Benchoona

southwest across the bog towards the stream, the lower part of which you followed at the beginning of the walk; look out for the interesting old stone structure on the far side of the stream. Turn right to follow the stream down past lovely pools, and rejoin the track alongside the river valley. Make your way past the concrete bridge and follow the path to the road and the car park.

Alternatives and Variations: The walk can be done in reverse by starting from King's Shop and Lettergesh Post Office (L749634), taking the small road on the right as you face the shop. When the tarmac ends, take the left track 200m along a right of way (past mobile homes) and over a fence. Follow the next fence to the right and cross the fence in front of you to climb up over a small spur. Then descend, cross the stream and climb a steeper second spur. Once on top of this, turn left and climb to summit of Benchoona. A shorter (but steeper) alternative for tackling Benchoona starts at the bend in the road between Lough Fee and Lough Muc, where there is a fine example of an ancient fort. Care should be taken to keep left of the crags under the summit. Descend from Garraun by the same route or via the west ridge to the south shore of Lough Fee.

9. DOUGHRUAGH AND LEMNAHELTIA

Introduction: This is a difficult-grade walk, with two mountains and beautiful lakes. It starts and ends at different points, so works best with two cars or lifts (the road between start and finish is very busy and can be dangerous). There are fine views of the sea and the surrounding mountains. This mountain features 'lumpy' igneous intrusion rock. There are options to omit the peaks. Nearby at Mweelin there is a megalithic tomb, holy well and a well-preserved limekiln.

Grade: 3 Difficult **Time:** 4.5 hours **Distance:** 8.5km **Ascent:** 820m
Maps: Maps OS *Discovery 37* and Harvey's *Connemara*

Start: L777587 Kylemore Lough lay-by on the N59, about 3km east of Kylemore Abbey. Park carefully in the gravel space beside the main road, opposite the lake.

Finish: L730586 Tullywee Bridge just north of the N59 between Letterfrack (about 2km west) and Kylemore Abbey (about 2km east). There is parking just north of/over the bridge near the gate, which is used by large vehicles.

Safety: Care is needed to avoid the cliffs around Doughruagh.

Route Description: Carefully walk west along the very busy main N59 road for about 150m to a gap in the hedge. Cross the fence and climb up north over the grassy moorland. Swing a little to the left (west), straight up towards the gently peaked outcrop that extends from Altnagaighera and Garraun. On the way you come to a flat boggy area, from which you head towards another waterfall, following the stream on your right. Your direction is with your back to the white house on the other side of Kylemore Lough, below Mweelin (or Benbaun). There are fine views of the Maumturks and the Twelve Bens, along with Doughruagh on your left (which you climb later).

When you reach the top of the broad flat spur, head north-westwards over the bog, past a small lake on your left and climb a little

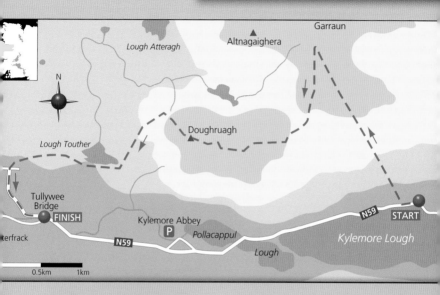

Kylemore Lough, with the Maumturks in the distance.

to reach the unnamed grassy mini-peak, marked as the 556m spot height. It is here that you get the best sea views, including Inishturk and further north to Clare Island and Achill along with nearby Altnagaighera (*Binn Fhraoigh*, and covered in Walk 8).

Turn around and head south, back along the ridge to the right of the lake, and descend in a generally southwesterly direction to the saddle at Lemnaheltia (*Léim na hEilte*: the Leap of the Stag). Notice a big white rock as you begin to drop down; this is a good place for lunch. Legendary warrior Fionn MacCumhaill's dog Bran is said to have fallen off this cliff after chasing a large stag from nearby Diamond Hill.

From the saddle, climb a little towards Doughruagh (*Dúchruach*: the Black Stack) and take the track heading left (south) for about 200m. Then leave the track to go right and start the steep climb in a westerly direction to the rocky moon-like summit, with its multitude of lakes and sub-peaks (take extreme care in mist). Be careful of cliffs to the south and further on to the north of this mountain. Continue to the west to reach the summit (526m) with a cairn and the remains of

Altnagaighera, with Ballynakill Harbour and Tully Mountain to the left in the distance

a rusty pole. From here you can see Inishbofin in the distance with the houses of Currywongaun (*Corr Uí Mhongáin*) – your next destination – in the foreground.

From the summit, head a little north of west for 300m. Then descend carefully along a spur leading northwest (avoiding dangerous gullies to the west, and cliffs to the north) until you are about halfway down to Pollacappul (*Poll an Chapaill,* the hollow or pool of the horse). Then turn to the southwest, towards an old stone structure below and onto the bog around the southeastern end of Lough Touther, which brings you via rhododendron bushes to the waterworks used to supply the Abbey.

Follow the stream heading west from the reservoir, keeping above it and passing some rocky outcrops. Continue along the sheep track as it passes smaller rocks and continues westwards. After 10 minutes you should start to see the houses of Currywongaun and drop down a little as you head to the right of stone walls marking fields. Keep the wall on your left – along with the stream – as you pass under a big tree to a gate in the rushes between two houses. Close the gate carefully. Turn left and follow the road for 700m to Tullywee Bridge.

Alternatives and Variations: This walk can be confined to lower levels (to be recommended in strong winds) by avoiding the two peaks; head straight to the saddle at Lemnaheltia, take the track to the right of Doughruagh and then to the left of Knappagh Lough and all the way around to Pollacappul, following the rest of the directions above. With a second car, you could drive to Creeragh Church (L799593) and start walking northeast along the N59 for 300m taking the small road on the left. Follow this to the end and climb the spur leading to Garraun, and on to 556m, before following the remaining directions above.

10. DERRYCLARE AND BENCORR

Introduction: This is an introductory strenuous-grade walk with steep climbing over very rough terrain in the famous Twelve Bens range. This walk requires fitness, a head for heights, and strong walking boots with good ankle support; the descent is quite steep. The walk features alpine plants, quartzite rocks and spectacular mountain scenery overlooking beautiful lakes. From Bencorr there is the option to continue around the Glencoaghan valley to complete a spectacular horseshoe and potentially the 'Twelve Bens Challenge'. The Derryclare woodland nature reserve – near the first part of the walk on the shores of Derryclare Lake – is a special stretch of native deciduous woodland where red squirrels are now thriving. First-rate fishing is also available at the start of the walk and other nearby sites.

Grade: 4 Strenuous **Time:** 5 hours **Distance:** 11km **Ascent:** 936m
Maps: OS *Discovery 37* (*44* for the first part of the initial forest road), Harvey's *Connemara* (useful for some details not marked on OS map).

Start/finish: L845499, which is the entrance to the Derryclare fishery/nature reserve at Cloonacartan on the R344 about 2.5km north of the junction with the N59 (2km west of Recess). There is a house on the opposite side of the road. The entrance has space for several cars, beside a gate and stile, but don't block them. Note that it is no longer possible to drive up the forest road.

Safety: Extra care is needed due to the harsh terrain, while the normal precautions regarding wind and mist apply.

Route Description: Enter via the gate/stile and walk the forest road for about 2km. The road takes you over two bridges, beside the beautiful Derryclare Lough; just beyond the first 1km, take the left fork in the road, go through a gate and then take the next (rough) road right (not marked on the OS map) up to a quarry. Climb carefully over the back of the quarry and into the open hillside, over felled forestry and past a few conifer trees to cross a fence. Climb up the small southern spur on your right – with the wedge-shaped rocky

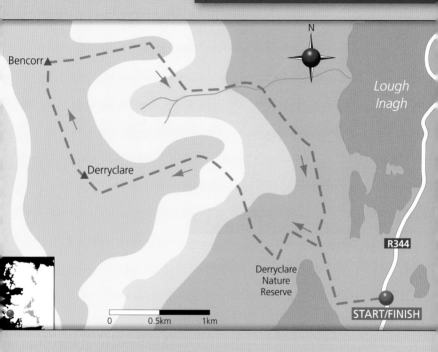

Derryclare and Bencorr Horseshoe

Bencorr

Derryclare

Lough
Inagh

R344

Derryclare
Nature
Reserve

START/FINISH

0   0.5km   1km

N

Lake in front of the summit of Derryclare, as seen from the north

knoll (*Eochair:* Ridge/Key, 190m) further away to your right. Take the grassy gully leading northwest up the mountain side. At the top of the gully, continue northwest before turning west-southwest to climb the rocky mountain side. The ground levels off and opens into a mixture of heather, bog and large quartzite rocks. It is a long slog (with several false summits), which gets increasingly steep and rocky as you approach the top of Derryclare (*Doire an Chláir:* the wood of the plain or plank, 673m) a little to the northwest. The views from here are stunning on a fine day; watch out for ravens.

From Derryclare you should descend, in an approximately north-northwest direction, steeply past a lake and down a ridge of rock and bog to a saddle (551m). Then climb the well-walked rocks to your second peak, Bencorr (*Binn Corr:* Pointed Peak 711m). This is the highest point on the walk and the second highest in the Bens; Bencorr was one of the original triangulation points used to survey Ireland in the 1830s, enabling bearings as far away as Tipperary and Kerry. It is said that northeast of the summit cairn there is an engraving etched into a slab by one of the original surveyors.

From Bencorr, turn right and carefully descend the ridge to the east over steep rocks and boggy heather for about 1km (the photo below shows this ridge from the northwest). Carefully begin your descent on the right-hand side of the flattening ridge, before the nose (which is dangerous and should be avoided). This steep ground brings you down into the valley (*Log an Choire Mhóir*, on Harvey's map). Keep to the right of the forest, making your way towards the stream flowing east.

Follow the stream beside the forest to make your way to a bridge. Turn right onto the forest road and pass Lough Inagh with its *crannóg* (ancient lake dwelling) and rare Arctic char. Continue along this surfaced road taking the left fork to retrace your steps past Derryclare Lough (this time on your right) and back to the start.

Alternatives and variations: In high winds or poor visibility, the Derryclare woodland nature reserve offers an interesting low-level walk, which could be combined with the wedge-shaped rocky knoll (190m; *Eochair* on Harvey's map) – overlooking Lough Inagh – northwest of the quarry. Derryclare and Bencorr represent the first part of another challenging walk: the Glencoaghan Horseshoe (Walk 12).

View of ridge descending from Bencorr with the Maumturks in the background

11. GLENCORBET HORSESHOE

Introduction: This is a strenuous circular walk taking in Benbaun – the highest mountain in County Galway. The total ascent is substantial with two hard climbs along with several shorter but still steep ascents. The walk features two impressive passes, fine views of several Bens' valleys, and a nice ridge. There is also a holy well nearby at Knockawaumgrean.

Grade: 4 Strenuous **Time:** 6 hours **Distance:** 12.6km **Ascent:** 1,085m
Maps: OS *Discovery 37*, Harvey's *Connemara* (useful for saddle heights not marked on OS map)

Start/finish: At L796573 where there is a group of houses (one with a velux window, opposite a modern stone-fronted house) just past the small track and a pole on the left: there is space for several cars to park in the gravel clearing leading up to a concrete water tank with a spout. Locals say this water is of high quality and there is a legend that the spring burst through to the surprise of a woman who had been poking around while minding her cows. The start can be reached from the R344, about 2km from the N59 junction at the northern end of the Inagh Valley. Near a bend on the R344, turn west at the small crossroads and continue for 0.7km – over the river Kylemore (*An Choill Mhór:* The Big Wood and the largest townland in Connemara) – past a stone-fronted house.

Safety: This is a difficult walk over hazardous terrain. Particular care is needed approaching Benfree and Benbaun (also descending).

Route Description: Take the old road/track into Glencorbet (*Gleann Carbad:* Valley of the Boulders or, possibly, Valley of the Chariots) for about 0.3km. When you get around a corner you can see the broad spur on your right leading up Minnaunmore: leave the track here and climb up to the top of the spur over the wet bog mixed with quartzite rocks of Illagarve. Cross the fences in a saddle where you can begin to see the Kylemore lakes and the sea to the northwest.

Glencorbet Horseshoe

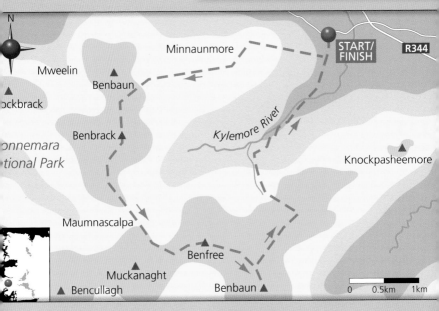

Minnaunmore

START/FINISH

R344

N

Mweelin

Benbaun

ockbrack

Benbrack

Kylemore River

onnemara
tional Park

Knockpasheemore

Maumnascalpa

Benfree

Muckanaght

Benbaun

▲ Bencullagh

0   0.5km   1km

Approaching Benbaun from the saddle with Benfree

Continue east to the first peak, Loughermore 392m, and descend to a gap. Climb the steep grassy hill in front of you to the southwest – crossing another broken-down fence, and passing several mini-cairns and outcrops – to the rocky ridge (from Benbaun, to the right, which you do not need to climb). When you reach the ridge, turn left and head south with fine valley views, taking the rough track up to the rocky moonscape of Benbrack (*Binn Bhreac:* Speckled Mountain, 582m) with several cairns. The cairn to the southwest marks the summit.

Take care descending – first southwestwards and then southeastwards – to Maumnascalpa, avoiding the cliffs on the right overlooking the westerly valley of *An Gleann Mór* (on Harvey's). Notice the steep northern face of Muckanaght (*Meacanach*) – fertile all the way to the summit due to its schist geology.

From Maumnascalpa, climb up – a little to the left of Muckanaght and past a small cave – in a southeasterly direction. Join a track leading to the saddle at 475m where the Glencorbet farmers used to take their cattle en route to Clifden mart. At the saddle, turn left and climb up the grassy track to Benfree (*Binn Fhraoigh:* Heather Peak, 638m with cairn).

From Benfree, descend to the grassy spur to a small saddle (583m) – in an east-southeasterly direction – and climb the steep ridge along an increasingly rocky scree track that bends to the south to reach Benbaun (*Binn Bhán:* white peak, 729m, with a large enclosure/cairn). All the main ridges in the Twelve Bens radiate from this summit.

From the summit of Benbaun, retrace your steps descending gently for about 250m, before turning right (beside a small cairn) to carefully descend the loose rocky scree track – in a north-northeasterly direction. Keep slightly to the left of a spur to reach a hummocky area that opens out into a flat boggy saddle near the lake south of the 456m knoll at Lugrevagh. Turn left here and descend – initially in a northwesterly direction – to pick up a beautiful stream. Keep the stream on your left and follow it as it swings around to the north towards a small house with a grey corrugated roof.

Make your way past this house to join the track leading down by the river. On the way you will pass the ruins of several old houses – one of which (on the left) – has several large flat stones outside that were smoothed by former inhabitants who passed many hours standing on them to chat to neighbours. Follow the old road along the Kylemore River to the crossing near a collapsed bridge; take care crossing and go downstream if there has been a lot of rain. Continue along the old road to the end to reach the car-parking area.

Alternatives and Variations: The walk can be shortened (to about 4.5–5 hours) to focus solely on Benfree and Benbaun by continuing on the old road along the river and up the valley to the saddle at 475m between Muckanaght and Benfree. It can also be extended to include the second (or northern) Benbaun (*Maolan*) peak after reaching Loughermore (add 20 minutes), Muckanaght (from Maumnascalpa, add 30 minutes and prepare for very steep, slippery climbing) or to include Knockpasheemore (*Binn Charrach:* scabby peak) at the southeastern end of the valley (add 25 minutes). The Gleninagh Horseshoe is a similar alternative to Glencorbet, taking in Benbaun, Bencollaghduff and Bencorrbeg.

Benfree with Benbaun behind, from near Maumnascalpa

12. GLENCOAGHAN HORSESHOE

Introduction: The extreme-grade Horseshoe of Glencoaghan (*Gleann Chóchan*) is one of Ireland's most dramatic mountain walks. With a total ascent of over 1,600m, covering six of the Bens, it is challenging and requires a very high level of mountain fitness and experience. On the way there are rugged peaks, scree descents and dramatic gaps, around glacial valleys. This is a not looped walk, so a second car or a lift will be required to return to the start.

Grade: 5 Extreme **Time:** 6–8 hours **Distance:** 14.3km **Ascent:** 1,660m
Maps: OS *Discovery 37* and *44*, Harvey's *Connemara* (useful for some details not marked on OS map)

Start: As per Walk 10 (Derryclare and Bencorr), L845 499, which is the entrance to the Derryclare fishery/nature reserve at Cloonacartan on the R344 about 2.5km north of the N59 west of Recess where there is space for several cars.

Finish: Benlettery Youth Hostel L777483, 9km west of Recess on the N59.

Safety: There are dangerous cliffs to be avoided (particularly Benbreen), climbs that require the use of hands (Bengower, Benbreen) and scree descents to be negotiated (Bencorr, Benbreen).

Route Description: Follow the instructions in Walk 10 (Derryclare and Bencorr) above as far as Bencorr.

From Bencorr special care is needed; descend gently to the northwest along the rocky ridge for about 300m and cross over the rocky wall after a gap. Continue in this direction for about another 100m (past a crag to the left) before turning left in a westerly direction, ignoring the spur to the right (653m, *Binn an tSaighdiúra*: Peak of the Soldier, on Harvey's), to descend steeply to the scree track leading to the saddle (494m on Harvey's; *Mám na bhFonsaí*: Pass of the Rims – or Pass of the Devil according to Joss Lynam). Take special care not to dislodge stones from the zigzagging track. The saddle itself is a narrow

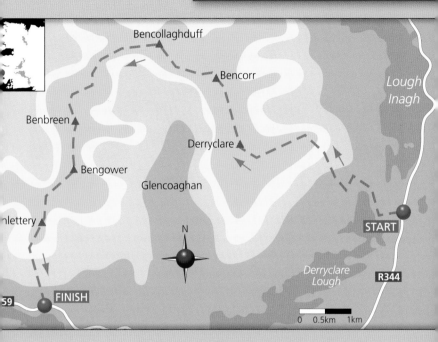

Glencoaghan Horseshoe

Bencollaghduff

Bencorr

Benbreen

Bengower

Derryclare

Glencoaghan

nlettery

Lough Inagh

START

N

Derryclare Lough

R344

59 **FINISH**

0 0.5km 1km

Glencoaghan Horseshoe from just northwest of Bencorr: (l–r) Benlettery, Bengower, Benglenisky (just visible), Benbreen, Bencullagh and Bencollaghduff (in foreground)

North side of Bengower, which requires the use of hands

boggy area surrounded by rock slabs; Carrot Ridge – Ireland's longest rock-climb at 370m – is to the north of here.

Climb the rocky slope in a west-northwesterly direction over solid slabs of rock to reach the grassy summit of Bencollaghduff (*Binn Dhubh:* Black Peak, 696m with cairn). You are now about halfway around the Glencoaghan Horseshoe. On a calm day, this is a good place for a break and to enjoy the view back.

From Bencollaghduff, descend the rocky spur in a westerly direction, zigzagging to the left to avoid crags at about 600m. Follow the spur to the left (southwest) as you approach the saddle at the head of the Glencoaghan valley (457m, *Mám Dearg:* Red Pass) above Maumina (*Mám Eidhneach:* Pass of Ivy, 407m). Look for ravens here.

Continue in a southwesterly direction, climbing the spur leading to Benbreen with its boomerang-shaped top and cairned sub-peaks. As you approach the top, keep left (east) to avoid a gully and then return to a southwesterly direction to follow a faint track below and around the left side of the crest at 686m. There are dangerous cliffs to the west. Follow the track around to the left in a more southerly direction with the crest on your right; on a still day, there is a good echo into valley to the east – near the 678m spot height – just before the summit of Benbreen (*Binn Bhraoin*, 691m).

From Benbreen, descend to the south-southwest (watching out for crags around the summit) and then directly south over steep and extensive scree to the saddle at 470m (*Mám na Gaoithe:* Pass of the Wind). Some people find 'skiing' or 'screeing' a good way to descend this.

From *Mám na Gaoithe* continue south to climb the steep Bengower (*Binn Gabhar:* Peak of the Goat). An obvious route becomes visible as you climb straight up. There is a short section where you have to use your hands and scramble – but the rock is stable and the climb is straightforward. When you reach the top go left (east) a little to reach the summit (664m) with cairn. From the summit descend to the southwest along a well-worn track to a small cairn at 560m. Turn left (south) and follow the ridge up to Benlettery (*Binn Leitrí:* Peak of the Wet Hillside, 577m; 'Bendouglas' on the OS map) – the most southerly summit in the Twelve Bens area.

From Benlettery, carefully zigzag southwest along a spur to avoid crags; there is a track, but you may need to use your hands on steep ground (see end of Walk 4, Bengleniksy, Bengower and Benlettery, for details). Follow the track in the bog leading to a fence in front of the youth hostel; cross the fence and pass through the beautiful remains of a deserted settlement. Keep right of the hostel to cross a stile to the driveway leading to the N59.

Alternatives and variations: Approach Derryclare from the road into Glencoaghan, via Lop Rock (OS map) and Bennaderreen Rock (Harvey's map); this will shorten getting/returning to the start. The Horseshoe can be walked in reverse, but the disadvantages include having to descend the northern rock face of Bengower and finish with a 4km forest trail. The Gleninagh Horseshoe is a slightly easier alternative to Glencoaghan, taking in Benbaun, Bencollaghduff and Bencorrbeg. An interesting alternative (Lynam, 1982) is a south–north walk from Benlettery to Kylemore.

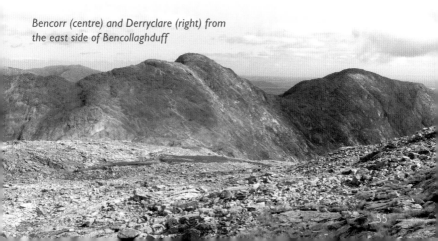

Bencorr (centre) and Derryclare (right) from the east side of Bencollaghduff

THE MAUMTURKS
AND JOYCE COUNTRY

This section includes seven walks, covering the complete range of difficulty. The easy walk (13, *An Seanbhóthar*) is on a relatively flat paved surface while the moderate walk (14, Lackavrea) is a relatively low but still challenging hill. The remaining five walks are medium to hard mountain walks, four of which (16–19) can be combined into a challenging traverse of the Maumturk Mountains, famously described by R. L. Praeger as a 'glorious day's walking'.

Although there is only one walk included from Joyce Country (13), this is an area with excellent walks in which good progress has been made to improve access (e.g. car parks around Benlevy). Several fine walks such as Bunacunneen, Finny Hill, and Buckaun have been omitted from this selection. Indeed efforts are under way to achieve European 'Geopark' status for this geologically exciting area. Joyce Country gets its name from the Norman family that arrived in the thirteenth century from Pembrokeshire in England; they pushed out the O'Flaherty's and over time became Gaelicised.

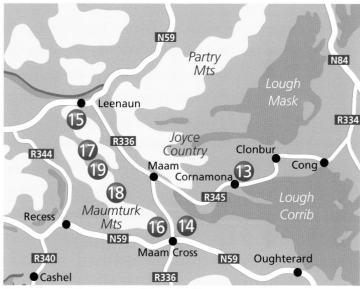

Maumturks and Joyce Country Walks 13–19

13. *AN SEANBHÓTHAR* (CORNAMONA TO CLONBUR)

Introduction: This is an easy linear walk along the old road (or *Seanbhóthar*) between two villages in a Gaelic-speaking area. It passes along the side of Benlevy (*Binn Shléibhe*, also known as Mount Gable) along a mixture of tarred and gravel roads – much of which is not accessible to cars – so comfortable walking shoes or sandals are sufficient (walking boots are optional). It has two very gentle climbs, fine views of Lough Corrib and passes an interesting archaeological site. The return to the start can be done by car/bike drop, taxi or walking.

Clonbur, at the end of the walk, has a beautiful wood (first right on the road to Finny Bridge and Cloghbrack, past the graveyard) with short walks and access to the spectacular limestone pavement. Further on, Finny has easily accessed world-class geology, sheep dog demonstrations and a lake beach. In the other direction, Cong has beautiful walks, an abbey, an unfinished canal and boat trips to the beautiful Inchagoill island (which has a cross pillar with the oldest surviving Irish inscription in Latin characters).

Grade: I Easy **Time:** 2.5 hours **Distance:** 8.8km **Ascent:** 230m
Maps: OS *Discovery 38*

Start: M038525, in the Irish-speaking or Gaeltacht village of Cornamona. Park on the road near the National School and Primary Care Centre. To shorten this walk, you may first leave a car (or a bicycle) outside the car barrier at the end of the *Seanbhóthar*, in Dooroy, (M088538) where unfortunately there is room for only one car (the local farmer may help); several cars can be parked in the car park on the main R345 road at M101541.

Finish: The village of Clonbur (M095558), where you can return to your car in Cornamona via a taxi/minibus (ask for numbers in the local shop, hotel or pubs).

The *Seanbhóthar* Linear Walk

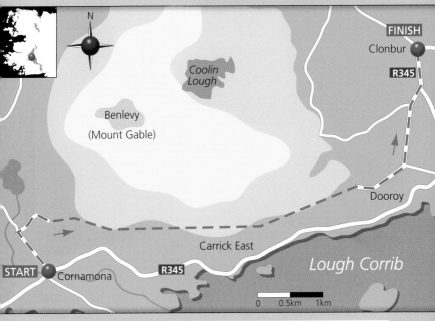

View of Dooros Peninsula and islands to the south of the Seanbhóthar

Ruined house near the barrier preventing cars entering the Seanbhóthar

Route Description: From the school, walk northeast past *Tí Mháille* and Lowry's Shop (selling food and maps). At the bridge take the small road on your left past the Post Office for 700m. Take the first road on the right – after you pass a '*Siúlóid*' sign at a bend – and climb the gentle hill past several ruined houses. On your left notice the lake back behind you (which has a *crannóg* or ancient island lake dwelling) and Mount Gable (*Binn Shléibhe* and Benlevy on the OS map).

After a beautiful ruined house and a road going to the right, enter the surfaced path of the *Seanbhóthar* itself, past the vehicle barrier. Continue along this ancient route that had eleven inhabited dwellings in 1901 and along which Irish was the spoken language. Notice the turf stands on the left and Ireland's second largest lake, Lough Corrib, on your right. Notice also the Dooros Peninsula with adjacent mini-islands and the hill of Derroura to the south, topped with an ancient cairn.

Continue along this road as it descends and then climbs to the townland of Carrick East. Near the top of the hill, on the left-hand side is a Bronze Age cooking site, (*c.* 1500 BC, a horseshoe- or kidney-shaped mound, with a green spot in the centre, known as a *fulacht fiadh*) near a small stream. Nearby on the opposite side is a grassy area with a children's burial ground.

Continue along the *Seanbhóthar* and exit past the barrier onto the small public road. Go straight/right here past some houses for about 1km, when you turn left at a fork in the road. Watch out for lovely views of Lough Mask and the Partry Mountains as you continue straight (ignoring a road on your left) for another 1.5km to the main road. Turn left here and enter the village of Clonbur.

Alternatives and variations: The route can be walked in reverse – starting in Clonbur and finishing in Cornamona. The walk can be shortened by leaving a car near the barrier at the end of the *Seanbhóthar*. A longer alternative is to walk back from this barrier to Cornamona for a total distance of 12km (3–4 hours). If you have left your car in the car park on the R345, when you exit the barrier at the end of the *Seanbhóthar*, take the road going straight/right and continue straight/right (ignoring the left turn for Clonbur in the main walk) and follow the straight road for another 700m to the main road. A similar level alternative is the Killary Famine Walk (L807625-L771648) over mostly unsurfaced paths.

Clifden-based archaeologist Michael Gibbons, at the fulacht fiadh at Carrick East

14. LACKAVREA

Introduction: This is a short, moderate-grade, looped walk at the southeast entrance to the Maumturks, overlooking Lough Corrib. The walk starts and ends gently but the hilltop is steep and rocky.

Grade: 2 Moderate   **Time:** 3 hours   **Distance:** 7.1km **Ascent:** 452m
Maps: OS *Discovery 45*

Start/finish: On the R336 at L974482, which is 3km north of Maam Cross (on the N59), where there is a gate, a stile and a signpost for the Western Way trail. There is room here for one or two cars; there is more parking in a lay-by just to the north.

Route Description: Go over the stile and take the small unsurfaced road that becomes a track with plastic 'mats' leading to a bridge. Cross the bridge and follow the trail – which becomes two planks over the bog – between the conifer trees. After the trail descends a little and turns a corner you will see Lackavrea Mountain through a small opening in the trees on your left; leave the Western Way trail here and go up this opening in the trees to enter the grassy open hillside through a hole in the fence. Head up north-northwest towards the mountain, passing the occasional rock outcrop and bush, as the view of Lough Corrib opens up on the right.

As the climb begins to steepen, and you approach the base of the hill, take the grassy gully going up slightly to the left. Follow this all the way to the top, taking care with the rocky final ascent to a flat area at 340m. This is the southeastern end of what is a long rocky plateau that undulates without a distinguishing peak.

Once on top, climb a little to the north-northwest for about 0.5km, over a mix of bog and rock, to reach the first of two cairns at 392m and 391m on rounded rocky outcrops. Notice the impressive thirteenth-century fortress Castlekirk (or 'Hen's Castle') on the small lake island to the northeast; this was one of the strongholds of the legendary Grainne (or Grace) O'Malley (*Gráinne Mhaol*), the so-called 'Pirate Queen' and leader of several Irish clans. Notice also Maumwee

Lackavrea Introductory Mountain Walk

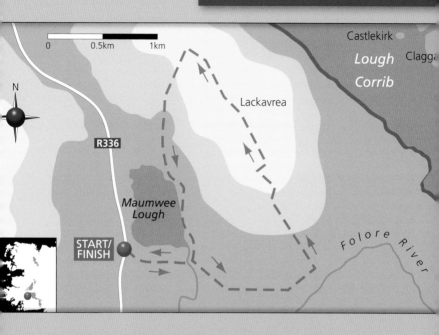

Lough flanked by Corkogemore to the southwest. Continue alongside a fence to reach the peak of Lackavrea (*Leicebhridh or Leic Aimhréidh*: Ragged Rock, 396m with cairn) on a heathery knoll.

Descend along the gentle rocky spur heading north-northwest (towards the 272m knoll) for a few minutes until you get to the flat grassy saddle. Turn left and descend over the steep ground, contouring to pick up a faint track and taking care to avoid bog holes in the long grass. Head for the small knoll (marked 88m on OS in front of the lake) and island. The descent takes you to a grassy valley with a rocky ridge at the far side and a track taking you left. Continue along the track towards the left side of the lake, crossing a stream before

Lackavrea from Claggan with Lough Corrib and Castlekirk in the foreground

a pebbly beach. Continue around the shoreline – rising above it at a steep corner – and past another pebbly beach. At the southeast corner of the lake, cross a fence and follow the stream on your right until you reach the bridge. Cross the bridge and retrace your steps to the road.

Alternatives and Variations: Similar alternatives to Lackavrea include Cashel Hill (L800437), *Cnoc Mordáin* (L864378) and Benlevy (M105549).

15. LEENAUN HILL

Introduction: This is an introductory difficult-grade walk from the picturesque village of Leenaun (also known as Leenane) beside Ireland's only fjord: Killary Harbour. There is only one climb at the beginning. There are excellent views and fences to guide you around the spectacular grassy and boggy crest. Note that Leenaun Hill is not named on the OS map.

To the south near Maam, the Glenglosh valley has interesting archaeological sites including *fulachta fiadh* (cooking sites), standing stones, a ring fort and a cave used as a hideout for a local parliamentarian during the Irish Civil War.

Grade: 3 Difficult **Time:** 4.5 hours **Distance:** 11.1km **Ascent:** 740m
Maps: OS *Discovery 37*, Harvey's *Connemara*

Start/finish: In the village of Leenaun, at the bridge at L878619. There are car parks adjacent to the fjord on either side of the bridge.

Safety: Care is needed when navigating the ridge in misty weather to avoid descending to the south. Occasional bog holes can also pose a hazard on the descent along with dangerous bends on the road back to the village (high-visibility clothing would be useful). Finally, there have been several landslides in this area in recent years.

Route Description: From the bridge in Leenaun, walk up the R336 road towards Maum. Continue for about 500m to cross a bridge – passing the Community Centre, a beautiful new thatched cottage, and the last house on your right. Enter the gate on your right and follow the track beside the stream and past the water tank as it climbs up into the valley revealing a lovely view back over the village. Continue up along a newly created track. Just below here, on the road to Maum, is the cottage of the infamous character Bina McLoughlin, a shepherdess who became known as the 'Queen of Connemara', and who had a large number of cats, donkeys, goats, dogs and a peacock.

Keep the fence on your left until it turns down sharply to the left, at which point you continue straight up before joining another fence,

Leenaun Hill Horseshoe

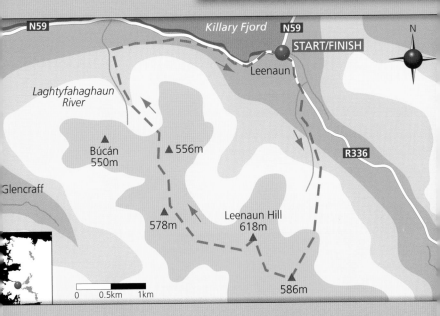

N59 **Killary Fjord** **N59**

START/FINISH

Leenaun

R336

Laghtyfahaghaun River

▲ Búcán 550m

▲ 556m

▲ 578m

▲ Leenaun Hill 618m

▲ 586m

Glencraff

0   0.5km   1km

N

The village of Leenaun, with flat moraine in front, on the shore of the Killary fjord, with Ben Gorm behind and Mweelrea to the left.

The cairn at Leenaun Hill, looking to the west-northwest, and showing the remainder of the ridge to be walked. The descent is from the saddle on the extreme right between Búcán (550m, with the light shining on it) and 556m.

also on your left. This fence leads all the way to the broad boggy top (586m, near *Meall Dubh*, on Harvey's). You have now completed almost all of the climbing. Take time to enjoy the fine mountain views in all directions.

At the top, follow the fence as it turns right along the flat, broad, boggy shoulder, in a generally west-northwesterly direction, past a small lake. Cross another fence, and turn right a little, in a more northerly direction for 350m to reach the summit of Leenaun Hill, with cairn: your highest point at 618m.

From Leenaun Hill, take a southwesterly direction to return to the fence, turning right and continuing with it on your left along the ridge. As the fence disappears downhill towards the Maumturks in the southwest, continue straight on in the same direction, to pick up another fence. Keep this new fence on your left, and continue past 578m (on your left) and a small lake towards the peak at 556m. This could be a relatively sheltered place for a break.

Descend in a north-northwesterly direction into the valley, keeping a little to the right-hand side in order to avoid bog holes. Notice the fine views of the fjord and surrounding mountains. There is a report in a German U-boat captain's diary of encountering a British submarine while sheltering in the fjord during the Second World War – but no fighting took place. Make your way across a tributary towards the Laghtyfahaghaun River. Cross two fences as you follow the river to get down to the Western Way – flanked by stones and with a gate and stile (no need to cross). Turn right to take the Western Way back to the road. Then turn right again onto the N59 back into Leenaun, taking particular care (get out your high-visibility gear) with the sharp bends as you approach the village.

Alternatives and Variations: This walk can be shortened by about 1 hour by carefully descending to the north from Leenaun Hill into the valley with the megalithic tomb and deserted village that leads to Leenaun. The end of the walk can be shortened by about 30 minutes by continuing to the north from 556m past the lake (nice for a refreshing dip) and carefully descending the steep hill in a northeasterly direction to the N59.

The peak of Búcán (left), the fjord of Killary Harbour with Inishturk on the horizon, and clouded Mweelrea to the right

16. CORKÓG

Use with Walks 17, 18 and 19 for complete Maumturks Walk

Introduction: This is a difficult-grade linear mountain walk, with three rugged peaks and a serious total ascent. The initial climb is tough, navigating the top can be challenging, and the final descent is steep and rough. You need to leave a second car at the finish, arrange transport back or allow 4 hours to walk back to the start. Note that the peaks are named on Harvey's *Connemara*, but not on the OS *Discovery* Maps.

Grade: 3 Difficult *Time:* 4.5 hours *Distance:* 9.4km *Ascent:* 976m
Maps: Harvey's *Connemara*, and OS *Discovery 37, 44* and *45*.

Start: At L965499 on the R336 about 4km north of Maam Cross (on the N59). There is a surfaced space for several cars on the west side of the road beside cabled poles and a post with a walker icon. This is just after the roadside fence goes uphill, about 600m after the R336 begins to descend from the top of the hill towards Maum Bridge (about 2km north of the Western Way sign at the start of the Lackavrea Walk).

Finish: L892495 in the car park at the west side of Maumeen. North of Maum, Glenglosh has interesting archaeological sites including *fulachta fiadh* (cooking sites), standing stones, a ring fort and a cave used as a hideout for a local parliamentarian during the Irish Civil War.

Safety: There are a lot of cliffs adjacent to this walk, particularly around the main peaks. In addition, the initial ascent and final descent are both very steep and require care. The flat, nondescript nature of these peaks can make navigation very difficult in poor visibility. The normal mountain risks of wind, and slippery rocks also apply.

Route Description: From the roadside, walk to the left of the mountain and a small ridge for about 200m across the rough grass until you reach a stream. Follow the stream right up into a small valley, crossing it before it emerges from a wall of rock and climbing up to rejoin it above. Continue to follow the stream up the heathery hill. When it disappears – as the climb gets steeper and rockier – zigzag

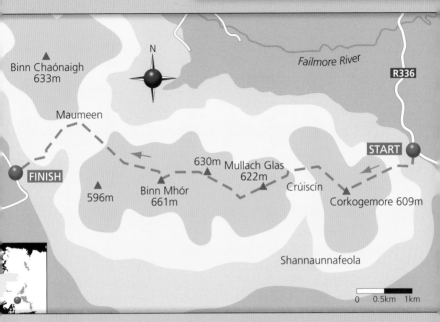

Corkóg to Maumeen West via Mullach Glas and Binn Mhór

Binn Chaónaigh
633m

Failmore River

R336

Maumeen

START

FINISH

630m
Mullach Glas
622m

596m

Binn Mhór
661m

Crúiscín

Corkogemore 609m

Shannaunnafeola

0   0.5km   1km

Fir clubmoss on the side of Corkogemore

your way up the slope in a west-southwesterly direction, avoiding the small rocky crags and using your hands if necessary. As this is a long steep climb, take time to look out for mountain plants and turn around to see the beautiful views of Lackavrea and the watery land behind you. If you reach an apparently impossible rock face, just continue to zigzag – with a greater emphasis to the left, from which side a fence eventually emerges.

Keep the fence on your left as the slope gets gentler, giving way to fewer rocks and more grassy bog. A small cairn appears behind the fence but there is no need to cross it (yet); the fence gets closer as you approach the summit of Corkogemore (*Corkóg*: Beehive, 609m, with cairn). On a clear day there are fine views to the east over Lackavrea and beyond Lough Corrib, while to the west and north the Maumturk range dominates.

If visibility is poor, it is better to continue down to the fence and follow it right down to the next gap. But if your day is clear, turn right from Corkogemore and descend along a rocky crest in a northwesterly direction past a small lake on your right. Keep descending carefully, staying about 100m above the fence (on your left) before joining it as it turns left. Once you join it, keep the fence on your left all the way down to the gap with the rocky hill *Crúiscín* (Little Jug).

At the saddle, cross the fence when it descends to the right (north) and follow the track right around the steep rocky knoll of *Crúiscín* (432m) to the gap overlooking the valley to Shannaunnafeola. Climb up the steep track to the right with old wooden stakes (fence poles); follow these wooden stakes all the way up to *Mullach Glas* (Green Top, 622m, with cairn and a small lake) – your second peak of this walk and a good place for a break.

From *Mullach Glas*, descend gently in a west-southwesterly direction to a fence in a grassy bog; cross this at a simple stile and continue in an increasingly westerly direction for 200m avoiding the cliffs on the right to the north (*Caobóg* on Harvey's map).

When you reach the top of a stony slope, descend northwesterly to the 520m gap (at Teernakill South on the OS map) with a stream. Maintain this northwesterly direction as you climb up the grass and rock hill – keeping left to ease the slope and avoid crags. At the top of what is your last major climb, a cairn marks the unnamed peak (630m) beside a small lake. Continue northwestwards along an undulating rocky crest past larger lakes. Turn into a more westerly curve to keep below a rocky ridge to the north and cross the plateau with mixed bog, rocks and grass. At a small grassy gap, climb southwest up to *Binn Mhór* (Big Mountain, 661m, with trig point); while not necessary, climbing to the rocky top rewards with fine views on a good day.

From *Binn Mhór* descend to the north for about 300m over a mix of rock and bog, passing some small lakes. Then turn left into a west-northwesterly direction (aiming for a point just in front of the 596m peak of *Binn Ramhar,* if visible) to take the spur for about 500m until the ground reaches an undulating plateau (at an altitude of about 575m) with large number of lakes. After you pass three lakes that are almost joined together – with the middle one surrounded by steep rocky outcrops – turn right into a northwesterly direction to carefully descend towards the next large mountain of the Maumturks – *Binn Chaónaigh* (if you can see it). A small cairn marks the descent, but there are no more lakes until you reach Maumeen below what is a challenging hillside.

Keep left of a rocky spur to the north as you carefully descend the steep and rough ground (a mix of rock, stones, bog and grass). As you make your way down, pause occasionally and look out for the lake below, keeping left of another rocky outcrop to the north; once you see the lake, you will soon see the chapel beyond. Descend towards the lake in a zigzag to avoid steep ledges of potentially slippery rock. When eventually all of the lake below becomes visible, complete your descent carefully to the left (southeast) end of the lake (avoiding the cliff directly above it).

Cross the bog, between the lake on your right and the 277m knoll on your left, to reach the holy well and chapel of Maumeen. This is a place of ancient pilgrimage to St Patrick (see Walk 18, Maumeen to Maumahoge). Turn left and take the stone track of the Western Way trail southwest down to the car park where your second car (or lift) should be.

This walk, from Corkogemore to Maumeen, can be used with Walks 17, 18 and 19 to form the complete Maumturks Walk which is a very challenging extreme-grade walk.

17. MAUMTURKMORE

Use with Walks 16, 18 and 19 for complete Maumturks Walk

Introduction: This is a long difficult-grade mountain walk. While the start and finish points are 20km apart by road, a circular alternative is possible. This walk forms the final part of the Maumturks Walk and includes the Maumturkmore Pass which names the range. The walk starts and ends gently on the Western Way trail, which can be wet, (plus a small section of road, which can be busy); in between there are two tough climbs over generally boggy mountains. There are beautiful views of the valleys and the Killary fjord. To the south near Maum, the Glenglosh valley has interesting archaeological sites including *fulachta fiadh* (cooking sites), standing stones, a ring fort and a cave used as a hideout for a local parliamentarian during the Irish Civil War.

Grade: 3 Difficult **Time:** 6 hours **Distance:** 15.3km **Ascent:** 931m
Maps: OS *Discovery 37*, Harvey's *Connemara*

Start: L859534 at Illion, where the small road east of Lough Inagh (off the R344, 500m south of the Lough Inagh Lodge Hotel) turns as it meets the Western Way trail (signposted). There is room for at least two cars to park carefully on the side of the road; do not block the Western Way.

Finish: L878619, in Leenaun village.

Safety: Strong winds can be a hazard on this high mountain walk and care is needed navigating in misty weather.

Route Description: Walk northwest along the Western Way trail for about 3km. The trail is clear, but it can be wet. After you have passed Letterbreckaun and crossed the bridge of the Sruffaunbaun River, turn right off the trail onto a less-used old grassy road that climbs gently to the north. Follow this old road as it narrows to a track around a small spur to a stream. Turn right and follow the stream east up the beautiful valley. Keep the stream on your right all the way to Maumturkmore (*Mám Tuirc*: Pass of the Boar). At the pass, notice the holy well (*Tobar Feichín*: Well of St Feichín) just over the fence (east), beside an old cairn.

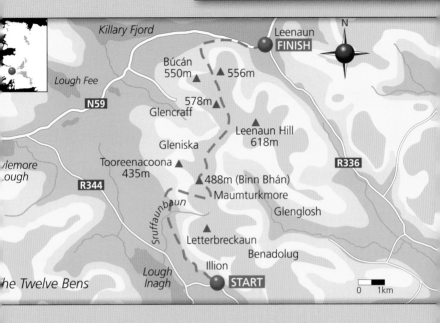

Killary Fjord

Leenaun **FINISH**

N

Búcán
550m

▲ 556m

Lough Fee

578m
Glencraff

N59

Leenaun Hill
618m

Gleniska

R336

Tooreenacoona ▲
435m

*Iemore
ough*

▲488m (Binn Bhán)
Maumturkmore

R344

Glenglosh

Sruffaunbaun

▲
Letterbreckaun

Benadolug

*Lough
Inagh*

Illion
START

he Twelve Bens

0   1km

From the holy well, climb up the steep hill to the north in a zigzag, keeping a little to the left. Follow the flat top left (northwest) past a little lake and climb up the rocky peak of *Binn Bhán* (488m, the OS labels this Maumturkmore). Descend a little to the right – ignoring the crest to the left for Tooreenacoona (435m, OS map) – and climb up over bog before joining a fence on the right and descending steeply from Gleniska. Cross another fence at right angles at a stile and turn right – keeping beside the fence – as you descend the grassy slope over another fence down to the saddle at 259m. This could be a good place for a break; the two valleys on either side – Glencraff and Glenglosh – are rich in archaeology.

Continue beside the fence up the hill from the saddle; there are a couple of steep rocky sections that will require the use of hands. At the top, cross another fence and turn left (north). Follow the fence on your left, continuing past 578m (on your left) and a small lake towards the peak at 556m.

Descend into the valley to the north-northwest, keeping a little to its right-hand side in order to avoid bog holes. Notice the fine views of the fjord and surrounding mountains. Make your way across a tributary towards the Laghtyfahaghaun River. Cross two fences as you follow the river to get down to the Western Way – flanked by stones and with a gate and stile (no need to cross). Turn right to take the Western Way back to the main road, then right onto the N59 for Leenaun. Take particular care (get out your high-visibility gear) with the sharp bends as you approach the village.

Alternatives and Variations: You can extend the walk about 40 minutes by starting north across the bog from Illion, following the stream right up to the flat entrance of the Benadolug hanging valley and turning left to follow the stream up to Loughaunnagrevagh and past Letterbreckaun to the holy well (see Walk 19, Letterbreckaun). Another alternative is to convert this into a circular walk by starting at the entrance to Glencraff on the N59 (L826612); walk up towards Glencraff and turn right onto the Western Way as far as Tallaghnamuinga and follow the directions above from the bridge of the Sruffaunbaun river as far as the Western Way where you should turn left to return to the start (with the possibility to shorten a little by descending earlier via *Búcán*, 550m to the west of 556m. The section of this walk from Maumturkmore to Leenaun can be used with the Corkóg, Maumeen to Maumahoge and Letterbreckaun Walks to form the complete Maumturks Walk, an extreme-grade challenge.

The rocky hill of Binn Bhán (Harvey's),
Maumturkmore (OS)

18. MAUMEEN TO MAUMAHOGE

Use with Walks 16, 17 and 19 for complete Maumturks Walk

Introduction: This is a strenuous-grade looped mountain walk that is also known as the 'Middle Maumturks'. It includes the highest peak in the Maumturks, *Binn idir an Dá Log* (Peak between Two Hollows). The walk starts off gently (a quiet flat road followed by a path rising steadily to a pass associated with St Patrick), before the climbing and navigation get tough, and it ends with a steep descent via a corrie lake into a beautiful valley. This mountain terrain is among the wildest in this book.

Grade: 4 Strenuous **Time:** 5.5 hours **Distance:** 12.7km **Ascent:** 1,050m
Maps: Harvey's *Connemara*, OS *Discovery 38* (note that the names of the peaks are absent) and *44* (for a small part around the Maumeen car park).

Start/finish: Park beside the bridge at L872521, south of Illion West (*An Uillinn Thiar*); there is space for one or two cars on either side of the narrow bridge. Alternatively, go southeast along the road for 4km to the car park on the west side of Maumeen (L892495; OS *Discovery 44*).

Safety: Navigating the peaks and the steep descent surrounded by cliffs can be very difficult and dangerous especially in poor visibility.

Route Description: Follow the road southeast along the Western Way trail. This Irish-speaking area of *Bun na gCnoc* (foot of the hills) is now virtually treeless although the place names (with many references to woods) and Lehanagh Lough (to the west, with trees on the islands) indicate this was not always the case. Continue on the road for about 4km past the school.

   When you reach the car park (L892495; OS *Discovery 44*) – on the west side of Maumeen (*Mám Eán:* pass of the birds) – turn left and go up the path through the gate. Follow the stony path for about 1.5km, passing the remains of a children's burial ground on the right, and continue up the hillside of Derryvealawauma (*Doire Bhéal an Mháma:* wood of the mouth of the pass). As you reach the pass you will notice small stone crosses and a building beneath a cliff on your left;

Maumeen to Maumahoge or 'Middle Maumturks' Walk including *Binn Chaónaigh* and *Binn idir an Dá Log*

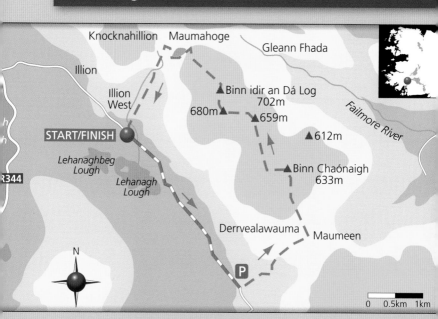

Knocknahillion   Maumahoge   Gleann Fhada

Illion

Illion West

▲ Binn idir an Dá Log
702m

680m ▲   ▲ 659m

Failmore River

▲ 612m

START/FINISH

Lehanaghbeg Lough

R344

Lehanagh Lough

▲ Binn Chaónaigh
633m

Derrvealawauma   Maumeen

N

P

0   0.5km   1km

The lake at Maumahoge in front of Knocknahillion

this marks the visit St Patrick is said to have made (without proceeding into Connemara). The site includes a small chapel, an open altar and a hollow in the rock known as St Patrick's Bed (*Leaba Phádraig*). Three annual pilgrimages – which have taken place here for centuries – are still held (on St Patrick's Day, Good Friday and the first Sunday in August). Continue a few metres east to the holy well (*Tobar Phádraig*, complete with objects left by recent visitors). Climb a little north to a second well, *Buntobar Phádraig Naofa*, and notice the fence beyond. Follow this fence northwest uphill; it is steep and rocky at times, but it will guide you safely almost to the top of this mountain.

Continue to keep the fence beside you on the right as you climb in a north-northwesterly direction. The hill is generally grassy, but it can be slippery and occasionally you have to use your hands at a rocky outcrop. After climbing steeply for about 15–20 minutes, when the fence stops at a sheer rocky cliff, go left over the grass for about 10m following the track up and climb up – using your hands – over the rocky outcrop to the right. Then rejoin the fence and continue to keep it nearby as it zigzags to the right. Rare alpine clubmoss, meadow-rue and juniper grow in these uplands. After climbing further up the mountain, at a grassy bog when the fence goes east and across the slope, maintain a northerly direction towards the natural slope of the mountain. This will take you to the lake that is overlooked by a cairn marking the peak. Care is needed in this jumble of shattered quartzite rocks, particularly if visibility is poor.

Continue north from the lake to reach the summit cairn – on a small white round knoll – marking the broad peak (*Binn Chaónaigh:* Mossy Peak, 633m). From the cairn carefully turn to the west – for no more than 300m – before picking up a track in broken quartzite rock going right and down. Take this rough rocky track down to the saddle at 523m, passing *Binn Mhairg* (612m) to the right and providing fine views of the Twelve Bens and the schoolhouse below in the valley on your left.

Climb north up the grass and rock slope. Follow the undulating ridge that takes you generally north before bending west to reach 659m; there is an easier route to the left of the ridge along a relatively flat track. When you emerge beyond 659m, switch to a westerly direction along a short flat ridge. There are fine views of the cliffs to the north down into *Gleann Fhada*. Climb up to the left of the crest to reach a small cairn at 680m (*Cnoc Doire Bhó Riada*), which reveals a spectacular view back towards *Binn Chaónaigh*.

Cross the grassy bog and rocky crest to the north and notice the views west as you climb up to the cairned peak of *Binn idir an Dá Log* (702m), the highest point in the Maumturk range.

Continue north over rocks to a flat peak with a small cairn. Turn left into a northwesterly direction to descend along a rough rocky spur for almost 1km. On the way the ground becomes grassier as you pass a series of small cairns that guide you along. Follow this spur as it descends more steeply and bends towards the right (north, avoiding cliffs on the left, overlooking the lake). Eventually (as you line up with the right-hand side of the lake below) a descending track becomes visible just to the left of an angled rock outcrop; go down carefully until you see the well-worn track of loose quartzite stones descending to the left. Carefully take this scree track down and across to the left hand side of the lake at Maumahoge (*Lough Mám Ochóige*). To the north there is a track that descends into Glenglosh, a beautiful valley that is rich in archaeological sites, including *fulachta fiadh* (cooking sites), standing stones, a ring fort and a cave used as a hideout for a local parliamentarian during the Irish Civil War.

Climb up the small hill on the south (left) end of the lake and pass through a small gap in the rocks to descend the grassy slope with a fence over to the right. Turn left and carefully descend through the grassy gap between the cliffs. Continue descending through rocks towards a waterfall on your right to join the stream below. Keep the stream on your right as you follow it down, crossing tributaries and past a smaller waterfall. Continue down following the stream on your right until it swings off to the left; cross the stream as you approach the electricity poles near the road above the bridge. Cross the bog to join the road and your car.

Alternatives and Variations: An alternative approach to these peaks can be made from the opposite side of Maumeen at L923519. There is room for a couple of cars here and the nearby bridge of the Failmore River. Walk up the Western Way to Maumeen and follow the description to *Binn Chaónaigh* and *Binn idir an Dá Log*. Instead of descending to the lake at Maumahoge, descend northeast and follow the Failmore River back to the bridge. The section of this walk from Maumeen to Maumahoge can be used along with the Corkóg, Letterbreckaun and Maumturkmore Walks (Walks 16, 17 and 19) to form the extreme-grade Maumturks Challenge.

19. LETTERBRECKAUN

Use with Walks 16, 17 and 18 for complete Maumturks Walk

Introduction: This is a strenuous-grade looped walk in the Maumturks. It starts gently before the tough climbing followed by a gradual descent to a trail, which is often wet. There are beautiful lakes, valleys, streams and mountain passes – including that of Maumturkmore, which names the range and has an important holy well.

Grade: 4 Strenuous **Time:** 6 hours **Distance:** 15km **Ascent:** 960m
Maps: OS *Discovery 37*, Harvey's *Connemara*

Start/finish: L859534 at Illion, where the small road east of Lough Inagh (off the R344, 500m south of the Lough Inagh Lodge Hotel) turns southeast as it meets the Western Way trail (signposted). There is room for at least two cars to park carefully on the side of the road; do not block the Western Way.

Route Description: Walk southeast along the Western Way road for about 2.5km, past the houses and over the small hill of Tonawausa. This is part of the *Bun na gCnoc* (Foot of the Hills,) Irish-speaking or Gaeltacht area. Turn left off the road before the bridge, and follow the stream up Illion West – crossing it as soon as feasible. Keep the stream on your left, passing several tributaries and small waterfalls, until it splits below a large waterfall; leave the stream here and climb up north-northeast over a few boulders to the pass at Maumahoge (*Mám Ochóige*, 347m). Watch out for mountain hares; they will scamper away if disturbed.

There is a beautiful lake up to the right, but you should turn left before the fence and climb the grassy slope to the northwest (which will give you a view back over the lake). Follow the increasingly rocky spur as it swings to the right before turning left (almost west and avoiding the crags) to climb steeply towards the rocky peak of Knocknahillion (*Cnoc na hUilleann:* Hill of the Elbow, 606m with cairn).

From Knocknahillion change direction, descending a little to the north over rocks past another cairn to reach the small pass, Maumean (499m, different from the more famous Maumeen Pass to the south)

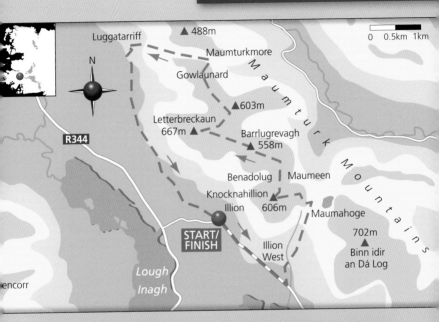

Luggatarriff
▲ 488m
Maumturkmore
Gowlaunard

M a u m t u r k

▲603m

Letterbreckaun
667m ▲
Barrlugrevagh
▲ 558m

R344

Benadolug | Maumeen

Knocknahillion
Illion 606m

Maumahoge

M o u n t a i n s

702m
▲
Binn idir
an Dá Log

START/ FINISH
Illion
West

Lough Inagh

encorr

0   0.5km 1km

N

Gowlaunard, Maumturkmore and the mouth of the Killary from Letterbreckaun with Mweelrea and the Sheeffry Hills in the distance

Approach to Maumahoge from Illion West

and continue up to the broad crest at 541m. Turn left (northwest) past a lake to a second lake (Loughaunnagrevagh) and take the track right to Barrlugrevagh (558m).

Continue northwest along the flat rocky ridge leading to Letterbreckaun (*Leitir or Binn Bhriocáin*, The Hill or Peak of Brecan, 667m). Go a little west, past some small lakes to reach the summit cairn where you should turn sharply right past another pool. Carefully cross big sharp rocks and descend northeastwards to another small lake (before 603m) – often a sheltered place for a break. The landscape softens here as the geology changes from quartzite to Silurian. About 1km to the east of here, at Gowlaunlee, a local public representative converted an old cave (possibly an ancient mine) into a hideout during the Irish Civil War, but the cave is very difficult to approach and find – even when you are right beside it.

From the small lake (L862554, near 603m) go left and descend gently in an almost northwesterly direction for about 700m along a relatively flat area that narrows. Descend to the right – across the slope – towards the boggy plateau of Gowlaunard. Go left around the bog and climb the rocks on the far side. Then keep to the right as you descend the steep grassy slope towards the fence and Maumturkmore, the pass that gives the whole Maumturk range its name (*Sléibhte Mhám Tuirc:* Mountains of the Pass of the Boar). To the east of the fence (beside a small clump of stones), are the remains of a holy well associated with St Feichín (also mentioned in Walk 1, Omey).

From the Maumturkmore Pass, turn left and descend the valley to the west. Follow the stream until it reaches an old path at Luggatarriff (*Log an Tairbh:* Hollow of the Bull). Take this track left and follow it around a spur and down right along a fence to join the Western Way at a stile; turn left onto the Western Way trail (which can be wet), taking it all the way back to where you started at Illion.

Alternatives and Variations: There are two straightforward options that will shorten this walk by about 30 minutes each: omit Knocknahillion and start by walking north across the bog from Illion, following the stream right up to the flat entrance of the Benadolug hanging valley below Maumean and turning left to follow the stream up to Loughaunnagrevagh; From the lake (L862554) northeast of Letterbreckaun, descend to the northwest along the Sruffaunbaun stream (and *Log na gCapall:* the Hollow of the Horses) to the Western Way. To extend the walk, continue from Maumturkmore to Gleniska and descend northwest along the spur, past the standing stone and fort, to the Western Way and return (along Lettershanbally – *Leitir Shanbhaile:* old village hillside) to the start. A further extension is to finish in Leenaun by following the directions for the Maumturkmore walk. The section of this walk from Maumahoge to Maumturkmore can be combined with the Corkóg, Maumeen to Maumahoge and Maumturkmore walks to complete the extreme-grade Maumturks challenge.

SOUTH MAYO

The coast is a strong feature in most of the walks in this South Mayo section. There are two beautiful island walks (21, Inishturk; 22, Clare Island) along with a superb beach system (20, Silver and White Strands). Two of the remaining mountain walks are beside the sea: the moderately difficult Croagh Patrick (23) is the most-walked mountain in Ireland; Mweelrea (27) is the highest peak in Connemara and Mayo. Maumtrasna, Devilsmother and the Partry Mountains are good walks from this area that have not been included.

The mountain landscape in this area is gentler, with rounded, boggy tops as opposed to the rocky peaks of Connemara and the Maumturks. The mountains of South Mayo tend to get more snow than the others in this book.

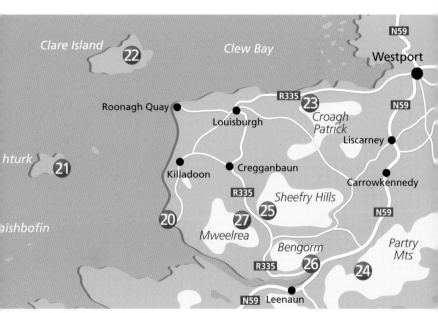

South Mayo Walks 20–27

20. SILVER AND WHITE STRANDS

Introduction: This is an easy coastal walk over two spectacular beaches (offering excellent walking in sandals or bare feet) and a connecting headland. This is a very remote and unspoilt area, with beautiful sand dunes, rare machair and interesting archaeology. The walk works best with a low tide. Note that on the OS *Discovery* map, the Silver Strand is labelled Trawleckachoolia, while the White Strand is simply marked 'Sand Hills'.

There are numerous archaeological sites nearby, including an old church site and holy well at Claggan, megalithic tombs and standing stones.

Grade: 1 Easy **Time:** 3 hours **Distance:** 9.5km **Ascent:** 207m
Maps: OS *Discovery* 37

Start/finish: L757683 at the Silver Strand car park 16km southwest of Louisburgh, at the very end of the small road south of Killeen and Killadoon. The last part of this road is narrow and can be busy on sunny holidays.

Safety: The main danger is high tides, which can cover much of the beaches and even reach part of the Silver Strand car park. It is best to set off on this walk when the tide is low; check the time of full tide beforehand. If the tide is high you will have to restrict your walk to the upper shoreline and take extra care. Swimming is possible away from rocks and the large White Strand stream, although there is a risk of rip currents. Care should be exercised along the Tonakeera Point shoreline – particularly if there are high winds or stormy conditions.

Route Description: From the car park, cross the footbridge over the stream and walk straight down the beach (Trawleckachoolia on OS map) towards the sea, as far as you can. Before you reach the water, turn right and walk along the shore to the grassy hill beside the rocks (above Keclawra).

At the western end of Silver Strand, go up the sandy track that becomes grassy and heads left up a the rocky shoreline; follow the

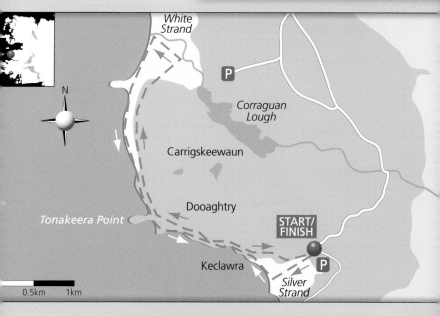

Silver and White Strands
Walk from the Silver Strand

White
Strand

P

Corraguan
Lough

N

Carrigskeewaun

Tonakeera Point

Dooaghtry

START/
FINISH

P

Keclawra

Silver
Strand

0.5km   1km

Rainbow over White Strand

track alongside some lovely pools with a wide range of marine life. Continue west along the rocky coast; cross a stream at a sandy cove beside a rocky outcrop, pass over boggy cultivation ridges (indicating pre-Famine settlement) and two large stones, which sit conspicuously on the grass, before crossing the remains of an old wall (partially covered in bog, suggesting it may be prehistoric). Keep inland of the shoreline on a vague track parallel to a line of stones on your right (the remains of another ancient wall) to pass more cultivation ridges and through a gap in another old wall descending from a large rocky hill (Dooaghtry) on your right; listen for a blowhole that you will pass when you return along the shoreline.

Cross a small boggy valley and take the grassy track up above Tonakeera Point jutting out into the sea to reach the corner of a wall with a wire fence near a rocky cove. Continue with the fenced wall nearby on your right, through a gap. After the fence turns right near a house with a gate, leave the fence and cross two small streams up to the small rocky hill overlooking the beach (a nice place for a break on a calm day). Descend to the grassy track just above the beach and follow it north. Your next target is the end of the sand dunes about 500m north; when the track splits you have the option to continue along the main track (keeping left of a fence after about 400m in Carrigskeewaun) – or take a minor track left staying closer to the beach through the marram grass.

When you reach the northerly end of the sand dunes, descend onto the beach and take a northeasterly direction towards a vague clump of stones on the beach (marked 'graveyard' on the OS map and across a stream that is currently further north). The stones are the remains of an early church and graveyard site that used to be inland of the sea (illustrating sea-level rise), which has been severely eroded since a storm in the 1990s damaged its walls. The position of the stream changes and it is currently beyond the graveyard to the northeast; do not cross the stream as its entry into the sea marks the point at which you turn south back down the beach. Assuming that you have reached the graveyard without crossing the stream, follow the stream in a northwesterly direction to the sea. There are good views out to sea, including Clare Island (north), Caher (northwest) and Inishturk (west).

When you reach the sea turn left and head south back along the beach. Away from the stream, the beach is normally reasonably safe for swimming despite a notice warning of rip currents. As you walk south down the beautiful beach past the sand dunes, the island of Inishbofin is visible on a clear day.

When you reach the end of the beach, cross two small streams and take the sandy track up the grassy slope to the rocky headland with a cairn where there are fine views. Continue south, keeping close to the rocky shoreline, taking care near the sea and watching out for any breaking waves. Pass the small sandy beach with various seaweeds at Tonakeera Point and continue southeast along the grassy shore past stony coves. Listen for the gurgling sounds from a wedge-shaped blowhole before continuing along a track and past another stony cove. Cross the stream again at the sandy cove and continue southeast towards the Silver Strand.

As you approach the Silver Strand, keep left to pass through the beautiful dune system above the beach (you could also return to the beach for a swim). Make your way east through the dunes towards the car park, passing under a large rock outcrop on your left and through a sandy gap to reach the large shell midden site. This includes a dog whelk midden on the edge of the eroding dunes (revealing evidence of extensive prehistoric settlement) – just before a post in a scattering of stones and shells leading to the beach and the footbridge to the car park.

Alternatives and Variations: A variation is to extend the walk by about 3km (40 minutes) by carefully crossing the stream in the middle of the White Strand and continuing to the end of the beach and back again. Another variation, provided the tide is low, is to start at the White Strand (car park at Corragaun, L744704) and save some driving; however, this requires wading across a stream that will be swollen by the incoming tide so you would need to start the walk before low tide. Similar alternatives to this walk include Carrownisky/ Sruhir strand (about 7km to the north, near the interesting Clapper Bridge Ford) and the tidal island of Finish (near Carna L778312 to the south).

21. INISHTURK (NORTH)

Introduction: This is a dramatic moderate-grade island walk over road, track, grass and bog. The main feature is spectacular sea cliffs, which present potential danger, are rich in bird life and offer challenging rock climbing along with superb deep sea diving. Inishturk (*Inis Toirc:* the Island of the Wild Boar) is home for a small community (about seventy people in winter). It also has some nice beaches, several interesting archaeological sites and Ordovician geology similar to Croagh Patrick. The rare endangered spotted rock rose (*Tuberaria guttata*) plant is found here.

Grade: 2 Moderate **Time:** 4 hours **Distance:** 8.4km **Ascent:** 490m
Maps: OS *Discovery 37*

Start/finish: L620749 at the main pier ('Quay' on OS map) on Inishturk. There is a daily ferry service (weather permitting) to the island from Roonagh Pier (L745808), 6km west of Louisburgh, County Mayo, where there is ample parking. Ferries are operated by Brian O'Grady (tel: 098 23737; mobile: 086 8515003) and John Heanue (tel: 098 45541; mobile: 086 2029670), with weekly services to Cleggan, County Galway (currently Tuesday and Thursday). Other boat options may be possible from Clare Island, Inishbofin or Letterfrack.

Safety: Care is needed near the cliffs, particularly in windy or wet/misty weather.

Route Description: From the main pier on Inishturk walk along the road (ignoring the small road to the right) for about 200m to the Y-junction and take the right fork. Climb up the road past the houses and go through the gate. Continue along the gravel road for about 200m. Go right off the track and carefully climb over a small hill and to the right of a large unfenced hole (very dangerous) up beyond the 85m spot height to see the marvellous cliffs of Garranty (summer home to breeding fulmars – a grey and white seabird with a yellow bill and good flying skills). Return to the track and continue along it

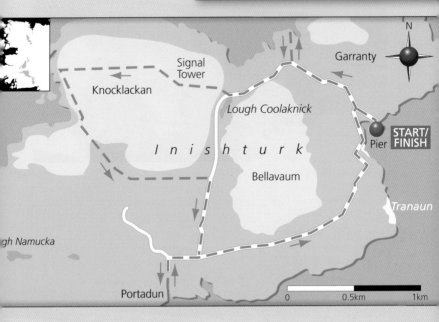

Inishturk Walk

Garranty

Signal
Tower

Knocklackan

Lough Coolaknick

I n i s h t u r k

Bellavaum

Pier

**START/
FINISH**

Tranaun

gh Namucka

Portadun

0   0.5km   1km

*Inishturk village and pier, with Caher Island
and the mainland in the background*

Béal na hAille *(Mouth of the Cliffs) from Knocklackan West of Mountain Common*

in a west-southwesterly direction to Lough Coolaknick (with nearby standing stone). About 100m past the lake, leave the gravel road in a westerly direction. Take the old track on your right, which will help you to climb the grassy slope to the Island's highest point at 191m, with ruins of the Napoleonic signal tower built in 1806.

Descend northwestwards for 300m, past several turf stands – stone structures previously used to dry turf (peat cut from the bog) used for heating and cooking. Then turn left to take a westerly direction and walk the 500m over the small hills of Knocklackan to approach the main cliffs, which maintain a vertical profile of 120–170m for almost 1km; be very careful.

After you have reached the cliffs and taken in the spectacular views, turn left and follow the cliffs at a safe distance from the edge, in a southeasterly direction. Descend carefully to the viewing point with a small fence. Watch out for peregrine falcons and puffins (in summer).

From the viewing fence, descend to the southeast and follow the small stream for about 200m (nearby are several early cooking sites or *fulachta fiadh*) passing a present-day, turf-cutting bog. Turn left before the stone wall, taking an easterly bearing for 500m to reach the gravel road. Then turn right down to the main road. At the main road turn right and after 200m take the small gravel road on your left and walk down to Portadun (*Port an Dún:* Port of the Fort) the magnificent natural harbour with a slit that was the site of early settlement – complete with *cillín* (another type of cooking site) and promontory fort.

Return to the road and turn right taking the road east all the way to the pier. Continue past the graveyard on the right (including St Columba's Oratory and bullaun stone), school (left), Tranaun Beach (right) and Community Club (left, with refreshment potential). There is a beautiful small beach on the way back to the pier, which is good for swimming. If the tide is low you can take the grass track opposite the electricity generating building that leads to steps down to the beach leading in turn to the pier.

Alternatives and Variations: The walk can be extended by up to 3 hours by continuing west from the viewing fence above the main cliffs. This will take you southeast to Dromore Head, past Lough Namucka, to Carrickavea, Drumnashargan Beg and along the south shore past Ooghduff to Portadun. When returning to the pier you can also detour to the graveyard and Tranaun Beach. Rock-climbing enthusiasts might be interested in *The Midnight Wall* and *The Razor Strap*. In addition to Clare Island (below), similar level alternative walks include Cashel Hill (L800437), *Cnoc Mordáin* (L864378), Mount Gable (M105549) and Devilsmother (L916625).

Portadun, the natural harbour with a very narrow entrance, the width of a small boat

22. CLARE ISLAND

Introduction: This is a difficult-grade walk featuring a special island with sea cliffs and interesting archaeology. The walk starts gently with a road climb and continues over grassy cliffs before the steep climb and descent to a bog followed by a road finish. A brisk pace is needed to complete the walk on a ferry day trip. The island has a population of 164 and is also home to significant numbers of breeding seabirds (fulmars and kittiwakes). The island has a fantastic heritage including Neolithic and Bronze Age archaeology, rare medieval wall-paintings in the fourteenth-century abbey, and one of Grace O'Malley's castles. The early 1900s' *Clare Island Survey*, by R. L. Praeger, is one of the most important natural history surveys in the British Isles.

Grade: 3 Difficult **Time:** 5 hours (this is at a brisk pace due to the ferry times) **Distance:** 14km **Ascent:** 742m
Maps: OS *Discovery 30*

Start/finish: L715852, at the main pier on Clare Island. The walk described is based around a day trip using the current ferry departure from Roonagh pier (L745808, with ample car parking) at 11 a.m. and departing the Clare Island pier at 5 p.m. The crossing takes approximately 20 minutes, so with a 5-hour walk there is little time to spare once you disembark. Prices are about €15 return but reductions are available for groups of eight or more. Ferry times vary, so you should check with the Clare Island Community Development Office, tel: 098 26525.

Safety: Care is needed along the cliffs from the lighthouse to Knockmore. The ascent to the summit is quite steep. There was a large landslide on the south east side of Knockmore a few years ago.

Route Description: From the pier, pass the ruins of an O'Malley tower house – Grace O'Malley's castle – and take the road to the right along the Blue Flag beach and then turn left (ignoring the turn immediately left). Keep straight on this road, over the bridge of a

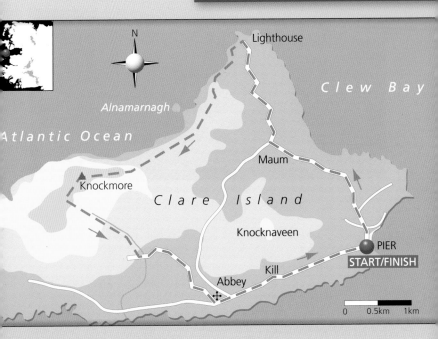

Lighthouse

Clew Bay

Alnamarnagh

Atlantic Ocean

Knockmore

Clare Island

Maum

Knocknaveen

Kill

Abbey

PIER
START/FINISH

0   0.5km   1km

View from the north side of Knockmore, along the cliffs towards the lighthouse, with Achillbeg Island and Corraun Hill in the distance

stream at Maum, until you come to a T-junction, where you turn right. Notice the standing stone on your left as you continue north up along the winding road.

When you reach the wall of the lighthouse (if it is not raining this can be a good place for lunch) perched high above the sea, turn left and go southwest along the cliffs. Follow the cliffs past Alnamarnagh Island and over a stream and swing into a more westerly direction. This is a great area for excellent field mushrooms. After you pass a couple of small knolls (spot heights 153m and 177m on OS map) climb up the spur to the south and then switch back to a westerly direction to climb the steep sides of Knockmore. Check your time and aim to have at least 2 hours to get from the summit to the ferry; if you have 2.5 hours from the summit you should have time to see the abbey's wall paintings.

The summit of Knockmore (*An Cnoc Mór*: The Big Hill, 462m, with trig point) has fine views of the neighbouring islands and mainland peaks. From Knockmore, continue southwest to a broad knoll before turning left and descending to the southeast. There was a major landslide to the left in 2007. There is a stream that will guide you safely to the road below. When you reach the road turn left and follow back it down towards the fourteenth-century Cistercian abbey, where you turn left onto the main road.

The abbey is worth a visit, particularly for the rare medieval wall-paintings in the chancel; the key is available from the nearby house. The abbey includes the O'Malley tomb where Granuaile may be buried. Notice the wall that curves around what is said to be the grave of a non-Catholic. There is a promontory fort a little to the southwest of here.

Take the main road left (east) towards the beach – past Kill and another promontory fort on the right and a 'mound' on the left – where you turn right for the pier.

The summit of Knockmore, the highest point on Clare Island with Inishturk (North) and Inishbofin in the distance

Alternatives and Variations: A variation for very fast walkers is to descend southwest from the summit of Knockmore to the signal tower, allowing at least 45 minutes to return to the pier via the road. A variation that would ease the time restriction is to arrange a lift to the lighthouse (try Bridget O'Leary, tel: 098 25640). Another option is to omit the cliffs and follow the track north of Knocknaveen, past Creggan Lough and up the spur past 219m to Knockmore. An easier variation that omits Knockmore and the cliffs would be to take this same track and climb Knocknaveen (223m), and visit the church before walking to the West End signal tower and returning back along the road to the pier. Alternative walks of a similar level to Clare Island include Mount Gable (M105549), Devilsmother (L916625) and Bunacunneen (L939578).

23. CROAGH PATRICK

Introduction: This is a difficult-grade looped walk along a ridge to the most-walked mountain in Ireland. Croagh Patrick is host to an annual pilgrimage on the last Sunday in July, when thousands of people climb 'The Reek' along a highly eroded trail from Murrisk (L920824). The walk described here starts from the west, climbing first to Ben Goram, following the ridge east to the holy summit before descending along the pilgrim's trail and returning via the main road. There are panoramic views including Clew Bay and the surrounding mountains.

Afterwards, you might like to visit beautiful Bartraw Strand, which is between Murrisk and Leckanvy. This area is also rich in archaeological sites: Murrisk has an old Friary and several standing stones; the Killadangan stone row, which is aligned on the winter solstice with a notch on Croagh Patrick is to the east; the Bronze Age 'cup and ring' rock art at Boheh (6.5km south-southwest of Westport) is also known as St Patrick's Chair.

Grade: 3 Difficult **Time:** 5.5 hours **Distance:** 14km **Ascent:** 890m
Maps: OS Discovery 30, 37

Start/finish: L873801 which is southwest of Leckanvy. Continue west from Murrisk on the R335, past Leckanvy for 1.5km, to take the small road left (L873820 with an Art Studio signpost). After 1km turn left up the small road for 500m to park on the right near a gate (do not block it).

Safety: Normal mountain hazards apply to the route described. Care is needed descending via the eastern pilgrim path with its loose rocks.

Route Description: Cross the fence and climb east over the heathery bog and stony ground up towards the ridge. When you reach the broad ridge turn right (southeast) and climb up; watch out for interesting small stone structures and notice the fine views back over Old Head to Clare Island, south to Inishturk and north to Achill.

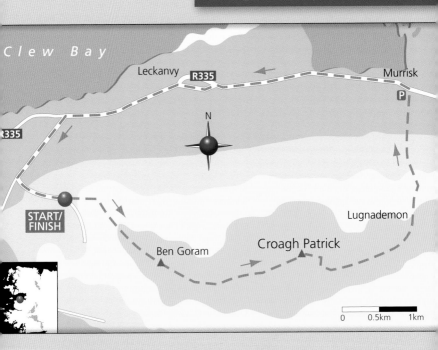

Croagh Patrick Walk

Clew Bay

Leckanvy R335 Murrisk

P

R335

N

START/FINISH

Lugnademon

Ben Goram Croagh Patrick

0   0.5km   1km

Continue up the increasingly rocky slope past a cairn with good views over Bartraw Strand jutting out into the bay.

Continue southeast up the rock and heather ridge past a small sub-peak up to the boggy top of Ben Goram (*An Bhinn Ghorm:* Blue Peak, 559m with small cairn). There are superb views from here on a clear day, including Croagh Patrick itself and the vast scattering of Clew Bay islands – glacial drumlins that were drowned after the sea levels rose following the last ice age, many of which now have eroded western cliff sides.

From Ben Goram, descend southeast a little to the saddle (488m). Then climb east, picking up the track that remains from gold mining activity in the 1980s. This track climbs gently towards three cairns at *Roilig Mhuire* (Virgin's Cemetery) where pilgrims used to walk around several times on their knees reciting prayers – following similar activities up on top of the holy mountain itself (Corlett, 2001). The final ascent to the pyramid-shaped quartzite summit is steep and rocky, but not nearly as eroded as the pilgrim path on the opposite side.

Follow the track all the way up to Croagh Patrick (*Cruach Phádraig:* Patrick's Stack, 764m), with church (where Mass is celebrated on Reek Sunday and other special occasions), various buildings and *Leaba Phádraig* (St Patrick's bed). The legend is that following fasting here for forty days and nights, St Patrick banished a flock of evil birds as well as the serpents of Ireland (the place name 'Lugnademon' to the northeast supports this story). About 20,000 people climb this mountain every year on 'Reek Sunday', many barefoot; thousands more climb it throughout the year. There is a suggestion that the pilgrimage goes back to pagan times.

From the summit of Croagh Patrick, take the highly sociable pilgrim path back to Murrisk. Descend to the east along the heavily eroded track, taking care with the loose scree just below the summit and follow it all the way down north to the car park at Murrisk (with visitor centre including cafe and shower facilities). Then take the R335 road left back to the start – via the minor road south around Leckanvy – and turning left at L873820 (signposted 'Art Studio') and left again to return to the starting point.

Alternatives and Variations: An extension is to leave the pilgrim path as it turns left at the L919803 saddle, and continue east over the 487m, 485m and 500m spot heights, to descend via

Deerpark West to the R334 near Murrisk Strand at L934821. A shorter variation is to return from Croagh Patrick back along the way you came, descending to the west and then west-southwest to the saddle (488m) turning right (west-northwest) up to Ben Goram and descending along the ridge to the northwest to where you started. An obvious variation is to start at the Murrisk car park and take the pilgrim path straight up and down. Another variant is to climb Croagh Patrick via *Tóchar Phádraig*, the ancient approach to the Reek that stretches 35km (longest of the surviving Irish pilgrimage routes) from the Augustinian abbey of Ballintubber and taking in many associated archaeological sites including Aghagower. Similar alternatives to Croagh Patrick include Devilsmother (L916625), Bunacunneen (L939578) and Maumtrasna (L973645).

Stone structure on the side of Ben Goram

24. THE THREE LUGAS

Introduction: This is difficult-grade mountain hike with a single ascent up a beautiful valley to a plateau overlooking a corrie lake. The walk descends to old oak woodland and finishes with a 4km road walk (which can be avoided with a second car).

About 6.5km south-southwest of Westport, there is Bronze Age 'cup and ring' rock art at Boheh (also known as St Patrick's Chair).

Grade: 3 Difficult **Time:** 5.5 hours **Distance:** 13.6km **Ascent:** 730m
Maps: OS *Discovery 38*

Start/finish: Take the N59 to 9.5km northeast of Leenaun. Park your car on the north side of Glennacally Bridge L935657. If you have two cars, you can drop one beside a ruined house just before Erriff Bridge (L960683), another 4km northeast on the N59, which shortens the walk by almost an hour.

Safety: Care is need with navigation on the featureless plain, particularly in poor visibility as there are dangerous cliffs.

Route Description: From the Glennacally Bridge, go through the gate on the right (closer to the river) and take the track leading upstream. Notice the beautiful clear water, rock pools, gorges, and waterfalls. There has been a proposal to dam up the entrance to this large bowl-shaped glacial valley as part of a hydroelectric storage system.

Follow the track beside the river to a flat area, keeping the fence on your left. When the fence turns sharply up to the left, follow it and notice the tributary – the Glenfree River – that is your new guide. This stream flows briskly through steep rocky gullies forming small waterfalls through narrow chutes in the sculpted rock. Keep the Glenfree River nearby on your right as you wind your way up the beautiful valley passing two streams. Turn left at a third stream (280m) and enter a small valley, following the water cascading down flat rocks back into the impressive valley.

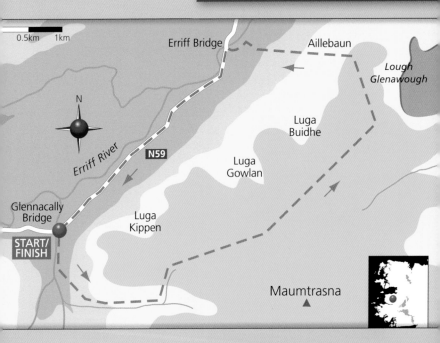

Three Lugas Circular Route

0.5km 1km

Erriff Bridge
Aillebaun
Lough Glenawough

N

Erriff River

N59

Luga Buidhe

Luga Gowlan

Glennacally Bridge

START/ FINISH

Luga Kippen

Maumtrasna ▲

The Three Lugas from Glennacally Bridge where the walk starts

The climb is steep now, as you approach the plateau. Continue to follow the stream though a mixture of bog, rough grass and rock, which eventually gets less steep as the full extent of the plateau unfolds. The top is very flat and featureless with only the nearby Loughans lake helping to identify the highest point of the walk at 621m. As the stream disappears, take a northeasterly direction and traverse the 2.5km of bog with occasional conglomerate rock. Notice the fantastic views in all directions. Take the gradual descent to the left bringing you to the cliffs overlooking the spectacular Lough Glenawough (*Lough Ghleann an Bhua*).

Go left along the undulating ridge above the lake towards what looks like a trig point. Carefully cross a rocky stream, and climb to reach the cairn on the 509m knoll. Descend gradually along the broad spur leading northwards (with Croagh Patrick visible to the left) and avoiding the crags leading down to the lake. There are great views of the Glenummera Valley and Tawnyard Lough leading to Mweelrea, flanked by Ben Creggan and the Sheeffry Hills.

Turn left to descend almost westerly. Continue to wind your way down near the scant remains of an old low wall. Descend towards the stream that joins the Owenmore River down near the woods. Cross the stream lower down – below the deep valley sides – and then head for the stone wall in front of the trees down below. Look back to see the hollow of Luga Buidhe to the south (a 'luga' resembles a large bite taken from a mountain, with the term often extended to name the associated peak – as in this case.)

Enter the atmospheric woods – keeping to the right of a fenced plantation – and make your way through the beautiful large oaks that are densely packed and surrounded by mosses and stones. Continue to descend beside the stream, which you cross near the river. Then follow the track parallel to the river, which will take you back to a ruined house adjacent to the main road, just downriver of the Erriff Bridge. Turn left and carefully walk the 4km back onthe N59 to your car (unless you have dropped one off beside the ruin). The reward for this road trek is that you get a proper look at Luga Buidhe (Yellow Hollow), Luga Gowlan (Hollow of the Small Fork) and Luga Kippen (Hollow of the Chip), the three peaks that give this walk its name, but are scarcely visible on the hike.

Alternatives and Variations: This walk can be extended by about an hour by turning right when you reach the ridge at the end of the plateau above Lough Glenawough. Continue along this ridge, climbing to Lough Naweelion on the westerly edge of the Partry Mountains. Turn left and head north for 0.5km before descending gradually to the northeasterly shore of Lough Glenawough. Then circumnavigate the lake underneath the cliffs and cross the smaller stream on the northwesterly corner. Contour around to Aillebaun and then down to the woods (as described above). A very long (8–10 hour) alternative, starting and finishing at Glennacally Bridge, proceeds as described above to Loughans before climbing south-southeast to Maumtrasna (673m). Then switch to southwest – joining the Galway–Mayo county boundary – along the plateau to Knocklaur and then the easterly ridge to Devilsmother. Complete the circuit via the northwards ridge back to descend to the Glennacally River.

Old wall leading to steep-sided stream (right) and woods below. The Erriff River is on the left, above which – in the distance – is Tawnyard Lake leading to Mweelrea and flanked by Ben Creggan (left) and the Sheeffry Hills (right).

25. SHEEFFRY HILLS

Introduction: This is a long, difficult-grade mountain trek, starting with a stiff climb and ending with a steep descent. But once the first summit has been reached there is little climbing, with two plateaus and a short ridge to be enjoyed before descending. The walk described requires two cars (or a pick-up; one car will make it significantly longer) with options to shorten it. These hills get a lot of snow. Superstitions are part of the folklore of these mountains.

Grade: 3 Difficult **Time:** 6 hours **Distance:** 13.1km **Ascent:** 880m
Maps: OS *Discovery* 37

Start: To avoid a long road walk at the end, leave a second car up the small road (signposted L1824, but not numbered on OS map) going east at the bottom of Doo Lough (also signposted for Liscarney, the Sheeffry Pass and cycling to Achill/Westport). A good place – allowing you options to shorten the walk – is the entrance to the forest on the left beside the Glenummera River at L872675. To start the walk, drive to L823699 approximately half way between Louisburgh (to the north) and Leenaun (on the N59) on the R335, where you can park near the Famine monument. This is about 1km north of Doo Lough, just above the small road going in along Glencullin Lough.

Finish: At the entrance to the forest beside the Glenummera River at L872675, where you parked your second car up the small road L1824. Alternatively, walk back along the L1824 road to the monument where you started.

Safety: The terrain on the plateau is rather featureless, making navigation potentially difficult in poor visibility.

Route Description: From the Famine monument, head northeast across the bog and climb the spur. Once on top, turn right and follow this spur as it rises (there is a convenient sheep track just below its top) and becomes more easterly in direction. Notice the old stone structure below, in line with Glencullin Lough. The climb steepens

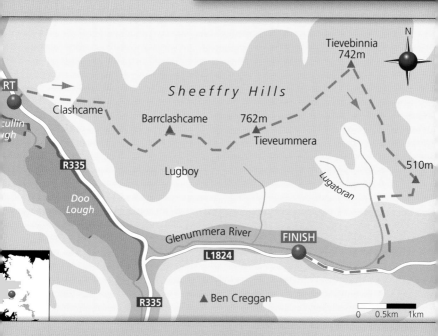

Tievebinnia
742m

Sheeffry Hills

Clashcame

Barrclashcame

762m

Tieveummera

R335

510m

Lugboy

Lugatoran

Doo
Lough

Glenummera River

FINISH

L1824

R335

▲ Ben Creggan

0   0.5km   1km

*View of Sheeffry Hills (including approach ridge on left) taken from
the southwest side of Doo Lough*

as you work up to the first peak above Clashcame, a good place for an early lunch. Then descend about 40m to a small saddle before climbing the steep and rocky southeasterly ridge that winds its way anticlockwise to the plateau with fine views over Doo Lough (which has rare Arctic char fish) and the surrounding mountains (Mweelrea, Ben Creggan). Proceed a further 500m to the northeast to reach Barrclashcame itself (772m), with a small cairn on relatively flat ground, the highest point of this walk and on a clear day illustrating what lies ahead.

Descend to the small saddle to the east before climbing the exposed ridge that falls away steeply to the left/north (there is an escape route to the right into Lugboy). Then continue in anticlockwise direction – keeping a safe distance from the cliff on your left – to reach the Tieveummera Trig Point 762m (not named on OS). Looking at the photo below, it is lined up with the ridge ascending to the left from the saddle.

View from Barrclashcame showing the next stage of the walk and the final peak in the distance on the left

Descend a little, leaving the cliff, in a generally northeasterly direction across the slope and then climb back up a little to return towards the cliff at a small saddle. Pass two lakes (and several smaller ones), before climbing a little in a northeasterly direction – taking care to avoid dangerous crags on the left – to reach a small peak. Continue northeast for another 1km to finally reach the flat and featureless Tievabinnia 742m (unnamed on OS, with a very small cairn). There is a fine view of Croagh Patrick from here.

From 742m, turn back around to the right to head in a south-southeasterly direction (taking care to avoid the steep crags to the south, on your right) across a broad boggy plateau (towards the broad beginning of a spur). After 1km, the spur becomes clearer as it narrows and should be followed as it steepens suddenly and turns into an almost southerly direction. The spur flattens out again as you approach 500m. Continue along the relatively flat spur and over the small 510m peak at its end. Then descend carefully to the south, towards the edge of the mostly felled forest. Turn right before the forest fence, and head for the stream with its beautiful veined rocks and the occasional holly bush. Turn left at the stream, and follow it inside the forest fence, crossing another perpendicular fence where it meets the stream. Continue down along the stream and around another fence at a river ford and take the small road down, past an old footbridge. This leads to the L1824 road, where you turn right and walk down along the Glenummera River to pick up your second car if you have parked it here. Otherwise, continue to the main road R335 and turn right to get back to the monument and your car.

Alternatives and Variations: The walk can be shortened by about 2 hours by descending from the saddle to the east of Barrclashcame in a southerly direction to Lugboy and down towards the bridge of the Glenummera River below the farmhouse. From the Tieveummera trig point at 762m, there are two options to shorten the walk by about one hour: 1) Retrace your steps southwest for about 0.5km and descend along the spur that goes initially to the east and then to the south, following the river to the dwelling and road; 2) Descend to the east adjacent to the Lugatoran River and down through the (partially cleared) forest road. Another option – from the two lakes (between 762m and 742m) – that shortens the walk by about half an hour is to descend east-southeast to follow the stream leading to the Lugatoran River and on to the main L1824 road.

26. BEN GORM AND BEN CREGGAN

Introduction: This is a strenuous-grade looped walk taking in three adjacent peaks. There is a lovely ridge climb, two gaps and a small climb before the finish. The views are spectacular on a clear day.

Grade: 4 Strenuous **Time:** 6 hours **Distance:** 11.3km **Ascent:** 1,080m
Maps: OS Discovery 37

Start/finish: L894644 at the car park northwest of the bridge at the Aasleagh (or Ashley) Falls. This is the beautiful waterfall off the R335, about 300m from the N59 just north of Leenaun. To get a closer look at the waterfall, keep your boots on and cross the stile on the left of the bridge into a field and walk up the bank. Lord Mountbatten's brother owned the nearby Ashley Lodge, and was in residence at the time of the fatal Sligo IRA bomb in 1979.

Safety: There have been some serious landslides in this area in recent years. High winds would make this walk dangerous. There are cliffs and gullies to be avoided.

Route Description: Cross the gates at the back of the car park on the north side of the road and climb northwest up the wet narrow fenced area to a fence that you cross onto the open hillside. Continue up northwest through the rough grass tussocks as it gets steeper. When you reach the top of the spur, turn left and continue west and then southwest along Letterass to climb the steepening spur with a track. As the spur narrows into a ridge, it turns west again passing the remains of a recent landslide, visible below on the left towards the fjord. The ridge bends a little to the north as you reach the flat and increasingly broad boggy top. On top, head west-northwestwards – taking care to avoid the cliffs on your right – for about 1km; cross the stream (that leads to a natural 'dolmen' and climb gently to reach the flat summit of Ben Gorm (700m with two small cairns).

From the summit of Ben Gorm, continue west-northwest – avoiding the cliffs on your right – for about 600m. Then turn right, northwards, to descend to the saddle. Cross a couple of rocky

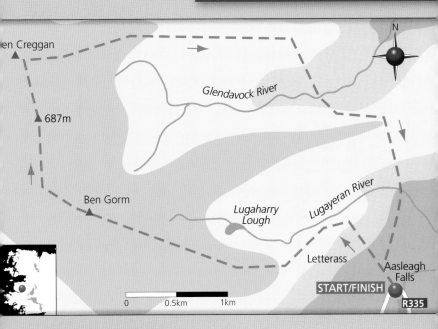

Ben Gorm and Ben Creggan from the Aasleagh Falls

en Creggan

▲687m

Glendavock River

▲ Ben Gorm

Lugaharry Lough

Lugayeran River

Letterass

Aasleagh Falls

START/FINISH

R335

N

0   0.5km   1km

Large (3m) dolmen-like stone perched just above the waterfall above Lugaharry Lough

outcrops as you climb up to 678m. Then descend over a steep grassy slope to a smaller saddle (with the ruin of an old shepherd's hut) before climbing up to Ben Creggan (693m), with its fantastic views of Mweelrea, Doo Lough and the Sheeffry Hills.

From Ben Creggan turn right and head eastwards (towards Tawnyard Lough) to descend carefully along the rocky spine. Further down this spur you pass a lake, which may be a good place for a break. Go down the grassy valley below the lake, until it heads off to the left where you should continue eastwards down along a spur. Shortly after this – at a height of about 300m – you should leave the spur and descend into the Glendavock valley on your right.

Cross the Glendavock River near a small cliff on the far bank. Pass a small circular stone structure before heading diagonally up and across towards a ledge on the left. Follow the sheep track that climbs gently in an easterly direction along the ledge above some rocks. Head up past a rocky outcrop towards the saddle. From the saddle, where there is a fine view of the Aasleagh Falls and upper Killary estuary, you should follow the stream south and pick up the sheep track contouring to the right before dropping down to cross the Lugayeran River.

Continue south, contouring across towards the clump of conifers; cross the fence and make your way south across the slope towards the top of the narrow fenced area that you climbed earlier. Cross the fence and descend to the car park beside the Aasleagh Falls.

Alternatives and Variations: Ben Gorm can be approached from Skirragohiffern further west along the R335, providing the possibility for a shorter walk by returning from Ben Gorm to Aasleagh Falls by descending east along the ridge (i.e. the ascent described above). Another possibility is to start the walk from the Glenummera River side, e.g. near Tawnyard Lough (taking the spur that starts with the 356m peak to the east of Ben Gorm). Ben Creggan and Ben Gorm can also be accessed from the Delphi side. Similar level alternatives nearby Ben Gorm include Devilsmother (L916625), Bunacunneen (L939578) and Maumtrasna (L973645).

Looking down at Doo Lough from Ben Creggan with Mweelrea (left) and Ben Bury (right) in the distance

Looking back up at Ben Creggan from the lake on the spur you descend

27. MWEELREA

Introduction: This is an exciting strenuous-grade climb to the highest mountain in Connaught (and the twelfth highest in Ireland). Its location – beside the sea, Killary fjord, and close to several spectacular mountain ranges – provides fantastic views on a clear day. But the summit is often covered in cloud and cliffs present serious danger. The walk described here is via 'The Ramp' from the northern end of Doo Lough; this route should not be attempted in icy conditions (two alternative approaches are outlined below).

There are a large number of megalithic tombs (Srahwee, Aillemore, Devlin South, Formoyle) and standing stones (Derryheeagh, Killadoon) in the area to the north. Srahwee (5km to the north, just west of the R345 at Cregganbaun) has a superb wedge tomb or dolmen dating from the late Bronze Age. This small but well-preserved tomb is right on the side of the road. The top was used as an altar during penal times and has a primitive incised cross at one end.

Grade: 4 Strenuous **Time:** 6 hours **Distance:** 12.7km **Ascent:** 890m
Maps: OS *Discovery* 37

Start/finish: L828695 on the R335 between the lakes (Glencullin Lough and Doo Lough) at Clashcame just south of the Famine monument. This is approximately halfway between Louisburgh (to the north) and Leenaun (to the south on the N59). There is room for several cars on the lake side of the road.

Safety: Mweelrea can be a dangerous mountain because of its height, cliffs and exposed location. Winds can be very severe. Care is always needed at the top of The Ramp, where the path becomes narrow above a deep gully, making it unsafe if you are uncomfortable with heights: the alternative approach from Silver Strand avoids this.

Route Description: Cross the bog between the two lakes by first heading towards the stream, crossing it via a makeshift bridge about 150m north of Doo Lough. Go towards the lake and through the gate on the right. Continue along the lakeshore past two small stony

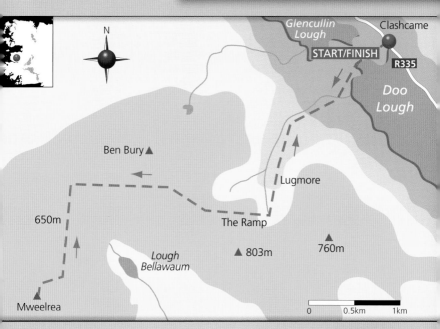

Mweelrea via The Ramp from the north end of Doo Lough

Doo Lough, near where the Mweelrea walk via The Ramp starts/finishes and the Sheeffry Hills Walk starts. The peak on the left is Ben Creggan (see Walk 26, Ben Gorm and Ben Creggan).

Lough Bellawaum in the valley below Mweelrea (the summit is to the left)

beaches and cross another stream at the far side (in front of the sheep pen). Climb the boggy moorland in a south to southwesterly direction, past boulders, up into the valley.

When you get to the brow of the hill at the valley entrance, keep your altitude and contour around to the left of the Lugmore Valley, keeping the streams and the centre of the valley on your right. There is a legend that Finbarra, king of the Connaught fairies, held one of his courts here. Continue into the back of the valley keeping to the left of several major streams and big rocks. Cross several steep mini-valleys (descending from your left), until you reach a large final one with a small waterfall. Climb up this mini-valley initially keeping its stream on your right and then crossing it to reach a grassy ridge on your right above a larger waterfall. Once above the larger waterfall turn right and follow the ground as it climbs steadily along the base of the ascending 'Ramp'.

Avoid the cliffs to the right and notice the wall of rock and towering cliffs above you on the left. Continue up through a clump of big rocks below scree under the rock wall on the left. Climb up the wide slope – past a minor peak on the right – and up the grassy track through stones. A steep climb close to scree on the left leads to another faint track. Continue climbing along this track, which narrows as a large gully appears on your right (and beyond it Ben Bury). Be very careful as it becomes very narrow and rocky. Continue up to the

Looking east, from the top of The Ramp, back into the Lugmore Valley and towards the start/finish point

grassy slope to the saddle with a small cairn.

Descend gently in a westerly direction for 1km – across between Ben Bury (on the right) and the cliffs above Lough Bellawaum. After a rocky area, turn to the south to reach the flat broad saddle at 650m between Ben Bury and Mweelrea (the easier approach from the Silver Strand arrives here). Then climb in a southerly direction – past the stone enclosure on your right – over loose rock to the grassy cliff edge above Lough Bellawaum. Carefully continue to climb just below the ridge (above the cliffs on your left) to reach the broad – and normally boggy – summit of Mweelrea (814m, with a small cairn).

Your return is via the same route. Start by heading north for about 200m and turning right to follow the cliff edge as it descends gently for about another 400m. Then leave the ridge to descend to the left (north) for about 600m to the broad saddle (650m) between Mweelrea and Ben Bury (the straightforward westerly descent to the Silver Strand starts here). From this saddle – particularly in poor visibility – care is required to safely reach the small cairn that identifies the top of The Ramp: start by climbing to the north for about 300m past the large rocks. Then turn right and take an easterly direction for 1km, to reach the small cairn: be very careful of cliffs in front of you as you reach this distance.

From the cairn, carefully descend – in a generally easterly

direction – to the faint track that leads down – above the gully on the left – to the top of The Ramp. Follow The Ramp all the way to the bottom. Then turn left and retrace your steps across Lugmore, past the beaches on Doo Lough, through the gate and back to the start point.

Alternatives and Variations: Mweelrea can be climbed in a variety of ways. An extended variation that features a beautiful ridge walk – but that should not be approached in strong winds – involves climbing straight up the spur from L844666. To take this approach, park at L845672 at where the R335 meets the lower end of Doo Lough. Walk across the beach, go in through the gate, cross over the weir and go in through the small gate. Follow the fence around to the left for 200m and then start climbing up to the right. Once climbing, keep slightly to the left as you carefully make your way to the top of a relatively flat spur that undulates up and down. Continue along this spur as you approach your first peak. The final steep climb to this peak, which takes about 15 minutes, is best approached from the left. On top, follow the spectacular grassy ridge to the left in a west-southwesterly direction, to the 760m spot height. Enjoy the views as you continue in this direction for another 500m, before turning right and descending in a west-northwesterly direction to a saddle before climbing to the 803m spot height. Continue carefully in this direction for about 700m along a spectacular undulating ridge peppered with

Looking down the approach to Mweelrea from the Silver Strand (right, with Uggool Beach to the left) along the Bunanakee River that leads to the saddle between the summit and Ben Bury

View from the ridge descending south from Mweelrea towards Killary fjord. Lough Bellawaum is below left. In the distance are the Maumturks (left), Lough Inagh (centre) and part of the Twelve Bens (right).

rocks. Then descend in a generally northerly direction to the saddle near a small cairn (above The Ramp), from which point you follow the directions above. This approach will add about 1–1.5 hours to climbing Mweelrea (each way, unless you return via The Ramp to a pick-up at the top of Doo Lough).

Arguably the easiest way to climb Mweelrea is to take the Silver Strand approach from the west. Park at Dadreen, L761685 near a bend in the road that leads to Trawleckachoolia/Carrickwee – known as 'the Silver Strand'. Climb up the lane, go through the gate (there are plans for a windmill) and turn right to follow a track to the southwest over a stream to reach the Bunanakee River. Follow this river left and up all the way to the broad saddle at 650m between Ben Bury and Mweelrea. From the saddle, follow the directions above. Returning by the same route the walk should take about 5 hours in total (about 9.5km, 800m ascent).

A final alternative (which works best if you have transport at the Delphi Adventure Centre) is to continue from Mweelrea along the relatively narrow and exposed ridge to the south. From this ridge it is possible to continue southeast to 495m and descend into the valley above the forestry where there is a track that leads to the Delphi Adventure Centre. This is only about 30 minutes longer than returning via The Ramp (provided you don't have to walk back to the top of Doo Lough!).

NORTH MAYO

This section covers six walks, all of which are near the sea. These walks involve very few fences, many of which have stiles. Two are low-level coastal walks (28, Castleaffy; 29, Inishnakillew and Inishcottle) around the shoreline and islands of Clew Bay, which require low tides for safe walking. Also featured are two spectacular coastal cliff walks (30, 33) and three mountain walks – ranging from difficult to strenuous. Two of the mountains (32, 33) are on Achill Island (which is connected to the mainland by a bridge), while the third (31) is in the least-walked range in Ireland (Nephin Beg). This landscape features extensive blanket bog.

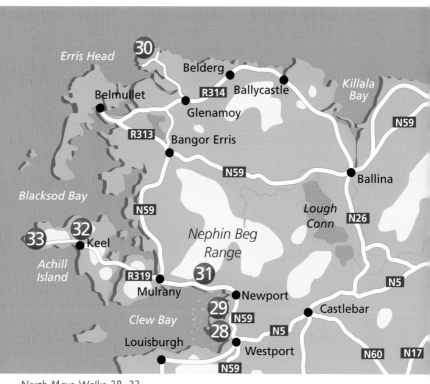

North Mayo Walks 28–33

28. CASTLEAFFY

Introduction: This is an easy low-level coastal walk that dovetails with the nearby Inishnakillew Walk (Walk 29). It should only be attempted when the tide is low: in particular, do not attempt if low tide was more than two hours ago. So if you start the Inishnakillew Walk 1–1.5 hours before low tide you could do this walk immediately afterwards. It features rocky coastline, a lovely old road, an impressive castle, a beautiful bay and a special bog.

Grade: 1 Easy **Time:** 1.5 hours **Distance:** 5.5km **Ascent:** 70m
Maps: OS *Discovery 31*

Start/finish: At the slipway L942883 on the north side of Castleaffy Strand. Be sure to park away from the access to the water and away from any boats. Castleaffy is 3km west of the N59 junction, about 5km north of Westport.

Route Description: From the slipway, walk southwest past several houses. When the road ends, take the left path to the shore. Continue along the shoreline as it swings around to the north – past Roscahill Point. Notice the large island of Collan More to the west, where Glenans Irish Sailing Club have a purpose-built sailing centre.

Follow the stony coast northeast to the small bay with an unsurfaced road. Leave the coastline and take the road left alongside a wall and follow it right past a special bog habitat. Continue along as the road degenerates into a track, and passes a beautiful old small house before turning right past newer houses to reach a T-junction. Take the 'bog road' on the right and notice the bulrushes. Go over the hill, descend to the bay and continue straight down to the Castleaffy Tower House (marked 'Castle' on OS map). This is a fine example of a tower house, a kind of fortified residence that was popular among the local chiefs in the fifteenth century. The cross-section nature of Castleaffy Tower House illustrates the standard plan: rectangular, three stories with a vaulted ceiling at first-floor level and passages within the thick walls.

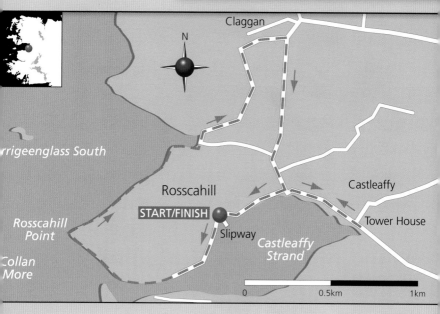

Castleaffy (and Roscahill) Looped Coastal Walk near Inishnakillew

Claggan

N

rrigeenglass South

Rosscahill

START/FINISH

Castleaffy

Rosscahill
Point

Tower House

Collan
More

Slipway

Castleaffy
Strand

0   0.5km   1km

Road leading to the slipway at Roscahill/Castleaffy Strand

Castleaffy Tower House

Small bay at Roscahill and road towards Claggan; there are remains of an old fort on the hill.

From the tower house, retrace your steps back and take the small road on the left alongside the shore to the slipway.

Alternatives and variations: For a short extension, take the small road left (north) beside the tower house for 2km to the Moyna holy well (just past the left turn). There is a local legend that this well was created when St Brendan changed the sex of an infant girl born to the wife of an O'Malley chieftain. The wife had escaped from an internal O'Malley clan battle on Clare Island in which many family members died, threatening the lineage.

The 'Famine Walk' along the southern side of Killary Harbour (L807625–L771648) is a similar level alternative to Castleaffy, as is the next walk (Inishnakillew).

29. INISHNAKILLEW AND INISHCOTTLE

Introduction: This is an easy flat walk around two small Clew Bay islands connected to the mainland via causeways. The walk is best approached just before low tide (preferably a spring/strong tide) and should not be attempted within 5 hours of a high tide. If you start this walk about 1.5 hours before low tide, you could follow it with Walk 28, Castleaffy, a short similar walk nearby. Much of the terrain is very stony, but the scenery is very beautiful, with fantastic views of all the islands and the mountains to the north. There are nearly 300 islands in Clew Bay, most of which are sunken drumlins (elongated whale-shaped hills formed by glacial deposition) – and one of which (Dorinish) was purchased by John Lennon in 1967.

Grade: 1 Easy **Time:** 2 hours **Distance:** 6.8km **Ascent:** 90m
Maps: OS *Discovery 31*

Start/finish: L944897, which can be reached from the crossroads in the middle of a straight part of the N59 about 6km north of Westport. Take the small road heading west with a sign for 'Seapoint House' (if coming from Newport, this is the second crossroads after the religious statue on the left, about 5km from Newport). Continue for about 2km to Claggan – past the new holiday home complex on the left and the Kilmeena GAA Club. After passing the fine patch of bulrushes on the left, take the minor road on the right (at the bend with a bungalow, before the Clew Bay Golf Club) past Seapoint House. Park near the new concrete pier on the right (do not obstruct it, the boats or the gates) – or continue over the causeway to park just 100m into Inishnakillew on the right.

Safety: At a high spring tide there is a risk of being trapped on the island for a couple of hours. Do not attempt this walk in high winds or stormy conditions.

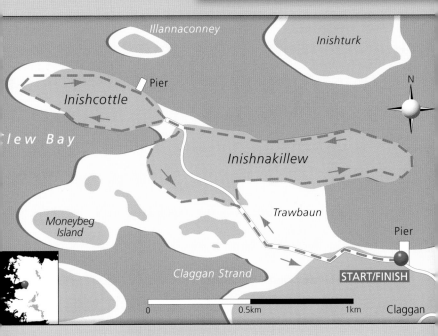

Illannaconney

Inishturk

Pier

Inishcottle

Clew Bay

Inishnakillew

N

Moneybeg
Island

Trawbaun

Pier

Claggan Strand

START/FINISH

0   0.5km   1km

Claggan

Inishcottle from Inishnakillew with (l–r) Illannaconney, Inishlaughil, Inishbollog and Inishmolt with the Nephin Beg Mountains in the background

Route Description: Walk out west along the causeway and past Trawbaun to Inishnakillew (population of three in 2006). Just after the causeway (and before the alternative parking spot), take the old track on your right through the ruins of a village. Continue east along the shoreline to pass some lovely small trees and picturesque fields to the end of the island. Continue along the stony shore around the eastern tip of the island, which passes close to Ross Point. Then follow the shoreline west alongside Inishturk (with its jetty and surprisingly large buildings). Pass the boatyard and join the second causeway leading to Inishcottle (population also three in 2006).

Cross the causeway and go left (west) along the shore, avoiding the small road up to the cottage (with noisy dogs). Watch out for the fossilised coral known as *Syringopora* – a quite finely branched colonial coral common in Carboniferous limestone. Continue to the end of Inishcottle and around the west end. Continue to follow the shore east and back to the causeway via a small pier.

Cross back to Inishnakillew and take the track on the right along the shoreline with handsome stone walls (alternatively you can continue on the road and up over the hill for a good view). Continue past a jetty to reach the causeway and return to the mainland.

Alternatives and Variations: The previous walk – Castleaffy – starts less than 2km away and can be added, provided the tide is right (see below) to give a moderate-grade walk. In fact, Castleaffy could be walked directly from the Inishnakillew parking spot, without moving your car. In this case it would be safer to do the Castleaffy walk in the opposite direction to that described in order to reduce the tidal risk; i.e. from the car park beside the quay take the right fork, turn right past the Golf Club entrance and take the road immediately right to the bay, and onto the shore following it anticlockwise around Roscahill to the slipway and tower house.

If you are interested in more challenging coastal walks around Clew Bay – but most of which require a strong (spring) low tide and thus extreme care, here are four possibilities: 1) Rosbarnagh Island can be reached by taking the small road west past Carrowbeg South about 1.5km south of Newport on the N59. Keep left when you reach the small bay and then take the right turn along the small road along Rosclave Channel about 1km past Rossantubble (where you can park). Walk the track over the hill (16m) and head out north to Rosbarnagh Island following the track west and north past hills of

34m and ultimately 37m. Return the same way. 2) Carrowcally can be reached by taking the small road west from the N59 just 1km north of Westport. Follow this for about 4km until you turn left at a T-junction at Rusheen School. Keep straight at the bottom of the road and after you pass Carrowcally, park where the road reaches the small bay looking out on past Rocky Island to Crovinish (with a few houses) and Beetle Island and Illanataggart to the northwest. 3) The Rosturk Islets can be accessible on a low spring tide from Rosturk Strand about 4km east of Mallaranny, south of the N59. They include the relatively large island of Moynish More, Black Rock, Inisherkin and Inishkeel. 4) The Drumfurban Islets are about 7km east of Mallaranny, south of the N59. There is a right turn about 800m east of Rosgalliv Bridge. These include Inishbobunnan, Inishgowla, Inishtubrid, Inishnacross, Beetle Island North and Inishlim (several of which have ring forts marked on the OS map).

Fossilised coral *Syringopora* (with 50-cent coin) on the shore of Inishcottle

30. BENWEE HEAD

Introduction: This is a dramatic, difficult-grade walk along a coast that is one of Ireland's best-kept secrets. It passes cliffs, crags, caves, chasms, arches, stacks and islands in a quiet Gaeltacht area rich in heritage. The views are spectacular on a clear day. The shale, schist and gneiss rocks of this coastline are very old, arising from Precambrian tectonic processes some 600 million years ago. The beach to the south of the start/finish point features extensive machair and the remains of the *Corrán Buí* sand hill settlement. Benwee Head features some good rock climbs.

Grade: 2 Moderate **Time:** 4 hours **Distance:** 12.1km **Ascent:** 420m
Maps: OS *Discovery 22*

Start/finish: At F820420, the *Seanscoil* ('old school') information centre in Carrowteige (*An Ceathrú Taidhg*), which has a car park, beside Garvin's shop and Post Office. Carrowteige can be reached from the R314 junction (signposted Ross Port) 2km west of Glenamoy (between Belmullet and Ballycastle); take this road northwest for approximately 12km (ignoring the turn left for Ross Port, centre of a controversial gas pipeline development).

Route Description: From the *Seanscoil*, head right (west) up the road (ignoring the left fork after 200m) past the school and pub (not obvious on the left). Continue along this road through a crossroads and down to a T-junction near Kilgalligan. At the junction turn right to reach the clifftop at the Children of Lir (*Clann Lir*) monument (at *Na Priosúin*). This sculpture (by architect Travis Price, assisted by architectural students from the Catholic University of America) commemorates the legend of four children who were transformed into swans by their evil stepmother, Aoife. After being condemned to live on the waters of Ireland for 900 years, the last 300 to be spent off this beautiful coast, they were buried on the nearby island of *Inis Gluaire*, one of the Inishkea Islands.

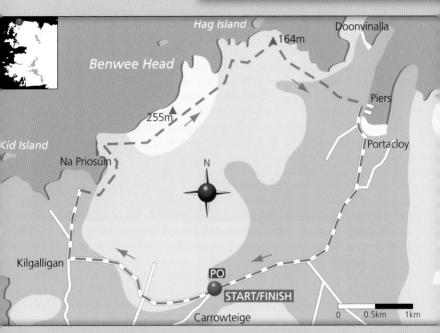

Benwee Head from Carrowteige via Portacloy

Hag Island

Doonvinalla

▲164m

Benwee Head

Kid Island

▲255m

Na Priosúin

Piers

Portacloy

N

Kilgalligan

PO

START/FINISH

0   0.5km   1km

Carrowteige

The cliffs of the bowl-shaped inlet Na Priosúin with Kid Island and Erris Head in the distance

Benwee Head with Hag Island and The Stags of Broadhaven

Follow the ditch east and then north, taking in the fine views back towards Kid Island (*Mionnán*) and further southwest over the Erris Peninsula to the Inishkea Islands. There are some good rock climbs on these cliffs.

Follow the ditch over a stream (ignoring the waymarks heading right) and then leave it to your right as you follow the clifftop left (northwest) and then right (east) keeping a safe distance from the edge; you start to get good views of The Stags of Broadhaven (*Na Stácaí*, a group of rocky islets rising to almost 100m with important bird life and superb diving). Climb up along a fence protecting the highest point of Benwee Head (*An Bhinn Bhuí:* The Yellow Peak, 255m) – provided you are careful, it is worthwhile crossing the fence for additional views, before crossing back over further along the clifftop.

Descend gently to the northeast along the clifftop overlooking Hag Island and north past another short section of fence before turning east again and climbing up towards the 164m spot height. At this point, turn to the southeast and descend gently along another dramatic clifftop overlooking Doonvinalla (with promontory fort: *An Dúna*) and Buddagh Island. Descend in a more easterly direction across a stream to pick up a track leading to the piers of Portacloy (*Port a' Chlóidh*).

From the pier (there is a short diversion out north along the west side of the bay) take the road right and immediately take the left fork though the scattered village of Portacloy (ignoring a road to the left) and up the road for 2km. At the junction turn right (west) to return to Carrowteige where you started.

Alternatives and Variations: This walk can be extended by about 1 hour by following the red and blue waymarked trail to the left, just 200m from the start. This trail will lead you all the way to the Children of Lir sculpture at *Na Priosúin*; passing the *Cill Ghallagáin* graveyard (with an early Christian Maltese cross stone slab), several promontory forts and the cliffs near Kilgalligan. A further extension from Portacloy could be to continue east along the coast to Porturlin, although this would require a potentially long road walk back to Carrowteige. A long alternative is to walk from Porturlin to Belderg which requires about 7 hours including the walk back by road. There is a fantastic selection of shorter looped walks available in this area: a guide, *The Dun Chaocháin Walks*, is available from the Seanscoil in Carrowteige; the *Siúlóidí Dorrais* guide is available from the tourist office in Belmullet.

The bay of Doonvinalla with Buddagh Island

31. BENGORM (NEPHIN BEG RANGE)

Introduction: This is an introductory difficult-grade mountain walk featuring a corrie lake. The walk has various options including extension to a long hard horseshoe or low-level looped walks suitable for poor weather. Near the start/finish point, the Salmon Leap Bridge is worth a look as it traps all salmon returning to spawn after their long migration from the North Atlantic (it is used for research purposes). Nearby there are interesting standing stones at Knockalegan (to the south) and Rosgalliv (to the west), an excellent castle at Rockfleet (formerly the residence of the West Mayo Burkes, originally the Anglo-Norman de Burgos and possibly where Gráinne Mhaol died) and the remains of Burrishoole Abbey.

Grade: 3 Difficult **Time:** 4 hours **Distance:** 9.5km **Ascent:** 550m
Maps: OS *Discovery 30*

Start/finish: L953982, beside a cottage, where there is room for a couple of cars just west of the T-junction at Lettermaghera South. From Newport take the N59 towards Mallaranny for about 5km and then the junction on your right (signposted Derradda Community Centre). Follow this road past the Derradda Community Centre (park here if you want to add 1.5 hours' walking on a lovely small road) and keep left at the Salmon Leap Bridge (where Furnace Lough and Lough Feeagh meet) to reach the T-junction.

Safety: The normal risk of high winds and mist apply. The cliffs overlooking Lough Doo should be carefully avoided.

Route Description: Walk west along the road over the stile at a fence and continue over another stile. Shortly afterwards (about 1km from the start), take the grassy track to the northwest until you meet a stream – turn right and head north-northwestwards up the open bog hill. Keep the stream on your left until it peters out, then head north to the saddle at 390m (a good place for a break). Enjoy the fine views back over the drumlin islets of Clew Bay.

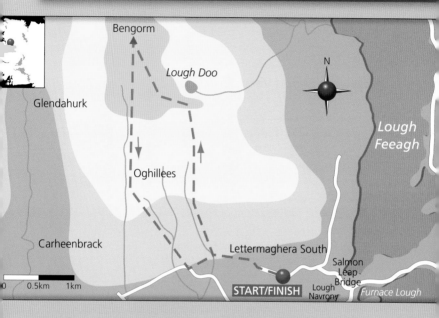

Bengorm Walk north of the N59 between Mallaranny and Newport, County Mayo

Bengorm

Lough Doo

Glendahurk

Oghillees

N

Lough Feeagh

Carheenbrack

Lettermaghera South

Salmon Leap Bridge

0   0.5km   1km

START/FINISH   Lough Navrony   *Furnace Lough*

Bengorm from the saddle overlooking Lough Doo, showing cliffs

Then climb – firstly to the northwest and then northerly – to the small cairn of Bengorm (*An Bhinn Ghorm;* the blue peak, 582m). Turn around at the peak and head south to pick up the stream at 430m. Follow this to the broad spur at Oghillees (230m). Find and follow the smaller stream down to the southeast. Cross the stream lower down – at a ford – to the reach the road. Go left and then take the small left track (near the looped walk sign). Cross the stiles to get back to the road leading to the T-junction.

Alternatives and Variations: To add an extra 1.5 hours of road walking, start at the Derradda Community Centre about 400m north of the N59 and follow the Oghillees Looped Walk (www.mayowalks. ie) past the Lakes (Pollagowly, Navroony) and return via the N59. Another possibility is to extend the mountain walk to various degrees by continuing northwest from the summit of Bengorm to the saddle at 357m and descending carefully into the Glendahurk valley (avoiding the forestry). If you want a long, hard horseshoe (approximately 8–9 hours, 21.7km, 1,630m), continue (past the 357m saddle) northwest past 468m and up to Corranabinna (716m, name from adjacent lake) then southwest along the narrow ridge to the east end of the plateau with 681m, then south along a sharp ridge to 478m and descending to southwest of Carheenbrack to join a track. This track is part of

the Knockbreaga Looped Walk that takes you across the Glendahurk river to a road from which you turn right onto another track (part of the Glenthomas Looped Walk) and pick up the return road below Carheenbrack. The 48km low-level Bangor Trail from Newport to Bangor Erris is a nearby alternative.

Lough Doo (left) and Lough Feeagh (right) from the saddle

View northwest from Bengorm showing the next part of the horseshoe extension

32. SLIEVEMORE

Introduction: This is a difficult looped mountain walk up and down a dramatic ridge and returning via road. The climb is steep and the terrain includes some rocky sections. There are spectacular views on a fine day and there isn't a single fence on this walk. Doogort Beach is normally safe for swimming, has beautiful sands and sometimes good surf. There is also good surfing at Trawmore Beach near Keel.

Grade: 3 Difficult *Time:* 5 hours *Distance:* 11.7km *Ascent:* 763m
Maps: OS *Discovery 30*

Start/finish: F672088 Doogort Beach (as on OS map and signs, often spelled Dugort). This is on the northern side of Achill, about 3km north of the R319 junction 3km past Cashel (with pub and petrol station). There is ample parking if you turn left (at a wall with signposts for the hotel) when you reach the beach.

Safety: With the steep drops along the ridge (particularly the east side), this walk can be dangerous in mist; watch out for changing weather conditions, which can be very rapid in Achill.

Route Description: From the beach, walk northwest beyond the hotel and past the last house. Leave the road and head up left over the grass and heathery bog to pick up a faint track heading up the ridge to the west. Climb up the increasingly steep ridge, taking care to avoid the crags, jagged edges and steep drops to your right. The track is intermittent, but the ridge to follow is clear.

Continue along the ridge that includes a couple of rocky sections, which are straightforward to negotiate provided you watch out for crevices. At the top of the ridge, continue west over a boggy plateau to reach the summit of Slievemore (*Sliabh Mór*, 'the Big Mountain', 671m with trig point). The panoramic view is stunning on a clear day: north to Blacksod Bay and Belmullet; east over the mainland; south to Clare Island, Croagh Patrick and Inishturk; west to Croaghaun and the Atlantic.

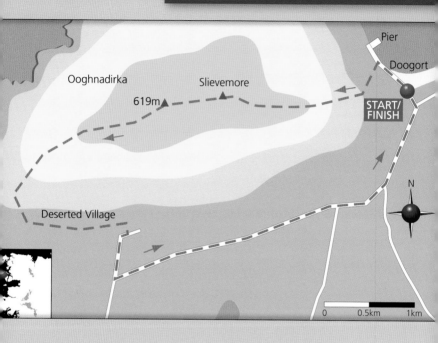

Slievemore from Doogort Beach

Pier

Doogort

Ooghnadirka

Slievemore

619m

START/
FINISH

N

Deserted Village

0   0.5km   1km

From the Slievemore summit, descend gently west for 0.5km to the sub-summit (619m). Continue west to pick up the ridge that descends steeply in a west-southwesterly direction to a plateau at 450m. As you descend the ridge, watch out for the interesting rock outcrops. Continue to descend to the west and then southwest. When you reach the base of the mountain, pick up a track to the left to the deserted village, which has a rich historical significance.

Continue past the ruined houses, along the recent track towards the graveyard. Turn right at the tarmac road and after 300m turn left onto the main road (signposted Doogort 4km). Follow this road past the sign for a megalithic tomb (a 10-minute diversion also offering an alternative route over the hillside back to the start), Puremagic B&B, kite-surfing school and pizza takeaway. Continue along this road past two road junctions on your right. Continue past the Heinrich Böll cottage (an artists' retreat) to reach the beach at which you turn left to return to your starting point.

Alternatives and Variations: Extend the descent from the 450m plateau by going north to the deep cleft in the mountain at Ooghnadirka before turning southwest back to the westerly end of the mountain. A long extension from the westerly base of Slievemore involves continuing west to the signal tower at 194m and all the way to 169m at Lough Nakeeroge before climbing up over Bunnafreva Lough west to 574m leading to Croaghaun (as described in reverse in Walk 33), but this would require a car/lift at Lough Acorrymore.

Slievemore from Bunacurry

For a shorter walk, retrace your steps from the summit of Slievemore east along the ridge to Doogort where you started. Another variation from Slievemore summit is to descend northeast and return southeast along the coast past to the pier and beach.

Megalithic tomb on the southern slope of Slievemore

33. ACHILL HEAD AND CROAGHAUN

Introduction: This is a strenuous-grade looped mountain walk featuring the highest sea cliffs in Ireland and panoramic views. There are no fences on this walk. But there are very steep sections to be climbed near exposed cliffs so this is not a walk for the faint-hearted. The beach at Keem, with its fine sand, is normally safe for swimming. Basking sharks were fished here with nets during the middle of the twentieth century. There is often good surfing at Trawmore Beach near Keel and other beaches, depending on the wind.

Grade: 4 Strenuous **Time:** 7 hours **Distance:** 14.3km **Ascent:** 1,169m
Maps: OS *Discovery 30*

Start/finish: F560042, the lower car park at Keem Strand, on the westerly end of Achill Island, past the villages of Dooagh and Keel. This is at the very end of the R319 which starts at the N59 just west of Mulranny.

Safety: Cliffs are a serious danger on this walk. There are very steep sections to be climbed near the cliffs, particularly on the ascent of Croaghaun and also along Benmore. Weather conditions can change very quickly in Achill; mist can descend rapidly around this exposed headland.

Route Description: From the southern end of the Keem Strand car park, take the surfaced path to the informative notice and then go immediately right up the track towards a ditch going uphill. Follow the ditch up and until it turns right, then leave it and continue uphill along a faint track south-southwest towards buildings. When you reach the remains of the old signal tower that was manned during both World Wars, take a look at the cliffs of Ooghdoo and Moyteoge Head; do not get too close to these cliffs – particularly if it is windy. Descend gently to the northwest along a vague grassy track, which runs above the earlier ditch; this ditch will be visible nearby over much of the next 4km.

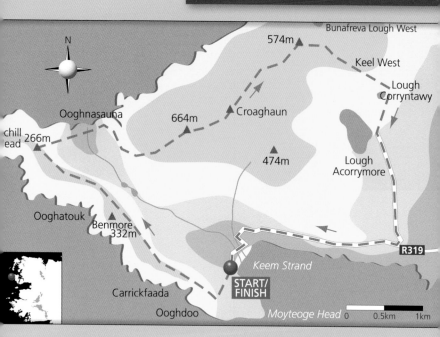

Achill Head and Croaghaun from Keem Strand

Bunafreva Lough West

574m

Keel West

Lough Corryntawy

664m

Croaghaun

Ooghnasauna

chill ead 266m

474m

Lough Acorrymore

Ooghatouk

Benmore 332m

R319

Keem Strand

START/ FINISH

Carrickfaada

Ooghdoo

Moyteoge Head 0   0.5km   1km

Keem Strand and Benmore leading out to Achill Head

View of Ooghnasauna and out to Achill Head

For the next 2.5km follow the top of the cliffs (or walk just east of the cliffs beside the remains of the ditch) to the northwesterly point at 266m. You will pass several viewing points that can be skipped if you are short of time. From the remains of the signal tower, continue along the track just below 296m and the rocky cliff edge before climbing up to Benmore (332m) where the cliffs of Croaghaun are spectacular (there is a shortening option here, see below); continue down the grassy track and then up left to 280m; continue down and past Ooghatouk up to 266m where you should stop.

In misty conditions be very careful to identify this point: as you approach 266m you should start to hear the sound of the sea on the right-hand side before reaching the grassy top with a small exposed bog, which is followed by a sharpening ridge to the northwest with jagged angular rocks overhanging the cliff and sheer, smooth, almost vertical slabs further west. This is a very exposed place. A clear view of Little Saddle Head leading out precariously to Achill Head is breathtaking; a 1.5km knife-edged pinnacle ridge (resembling a crooked index finger) stretches out into the Atlantic to the *Gaoí Saggart* and Carrickakin sea stacks. It is said that in 1968 two locals herding sheep found a crate of cold beer, lemonade, sandwiches and chocolate at this point. With nobody in sight, they helped themselves to a little refreshment, but did not dare to finish everything for fear it was fairies that had left the picnic. Locals now suggest the picnic was left behind by John Lennon and Yoko Ono who were staying at a nearby hotel with a helicopter (around this time, Lennon purchased an island in Clew Bay).

Turn right at 266m and descend carefully to the east with fine views of Achill Head and Croaghaun cliffs. Join the ditch and carefully cross a small stream at Ooghnasauna before passing a large vertical outcrop of white quartz on your left. Cross the steep-sided stream overlooking the epic seascape and ocean swell; this is a good place for a break. Here you can see that the 'ditch' has a stone base and is very old.

Climb up along the ditch and follow it along Bunown and around, up to the right of a cliff-cove with great views of the Croaghaun cliffs (on a clear day!). There are peregrine falcons living on these cliffs. Great care is required on the coming ascent due to the large sloping slabs of rock from which a slip would be fatal. Follow the ditch up until it disappears, maintaining a safe distance from the cliff edge, avoiding any crags and increasing your distance from the cliff edge as the hill gets even steeper. After you have passed the cliff, continue straight up the increasingly rocky mountain – to the northeast – to the pyramid-shaped 664m sub-peak with spectacular views of Achill Head. This clifftop is very dramatic – and dangerous, particularly in an easterly wind.

Atlantic Ocean below the cliffs of Croaghaun (right) with Saddle Head (left) in the distance

Continue down east from 664m – keeping safely clear of the cliff edge – and then up northeast along the clifftop to Croaghaun itself (*Cruachán*, 'Little Stack', 688m) with cairn and panoramic view.

From the 688m summit, descend northeast along the clifftop – again keeping a safe distance from the edge. Continue past 574m until you are directly above Bunnafreva Lough West (perched dramatically between the cliffs) and turn right (southeast) to descend gently to the rim over Lough Acorrymore (*Lough an Coire Mór*, Lake of the Big Corrie). From the rim over the corrie, carefully continue down via Keel West to the southeast keeping a safe distance from the crags on your right. Pass the smaller Lough Corryntawy before turning right (south) and heading across the spur to the road at the east end of Lough Acorrymore. Take the road down to the main road and turn right to return to the starting point along a geological boundary (between schist and quartzite-exposing seams of amethyst quartz in the nearby cliff).

Alternatives and Variations: If you are short of time the following options are available: omit the signal tower at the start by heading northwest to Carrickfaada (saving about 10 minutes); leave the Benmore cliffs at 332m turning right (northeast) to descend and cross the wet valley near two lakes, continuing straight up to Croaghaun (saving about 40 minutes); omit the Benmore cliffs altogether and start by heading up along the stream behind the car park, which

Remains of the Bunowna 'booley village' with Croaghaun behind in mist

Menawn Cliffs from Keel Beach (Trawmore)

passes the old coastguard station to the lakes from where you can climb straight up Croaghaun (saving about 1 hour); from Croaghaun summit descend to the southeast along the spur to 474m and either continue in this direction past 255m and steeply to the road (saving about 40 minutes) or at 474m turn right and take a southwesterly direction over very steep ground to pick up the stream leading to Keem Strand (saving about 1 hour). A much shorter version of the walk omits Croaghaun altogether but focuses on the Benmore cliffs: from the stream/ditch junction at Ooghnasauna (F541058) follow the stream up southeast through the remains of a booley village (where people minding livestock lived during summer months), past the lakes and down beside the stream to Keem.

An alternative approach to Croaghaun is from Lough Acorrymore car park (F578058) taking the direct route west via 474m or north past Lough Corryntawy and via Keel West. This approach to Croaghaun can be extended into a fantastic day-long coastal mountain hike by descending eastwards from Bunnafreva Lough, east past Lough Nakeeroge to spot heights 234m, 194m (with signal tower) and 89m before climbing northeast along the spur to Slievemore summit and down to the beach at Dooagh. Achill offers a multitude of other walks (a local booklet is available) including the 466m summit above the Menawn Cliffs (or the 403m minor summit with road access) from which the sunset is fantastic.

References

Corlett, Christiaan, *Antiquities of West Mayo*, Wordwell, 2001.

Dillon, Paddy, *Connemara, Rambler's Guide*, Collins, 2001.

Corcoran, Kevin, *West of Ireland Walks*, O'Brien Press, 2004.

Elliott, Joanne and Elliott, Eric, *The Story of Inishbofin*, Daisy Press, Inishbofin, 2007.

Harvey, *Connemara Superwalker*, 2000.

Lynam, Joss, *The Mountains of Connemara*, Folding Landscapes, 1988.

Lynam, Joss, *Irish Peaks*, Constable, 1982.

Mannion, K. (ed.), *Croí Chonamara – The Heart of Connemara: the History of Ballinafad*, Recess and Bun na gCnoc, BRB Community Council, 1998.

Ordnance Survey Ireland, *Discovery Series* 1:50 000 (particularly No. 37, 3rd edition, also 30, 31, 38, 44, 22, 23).

Ordnance Survey Ireland, *Trail Master* (version 1.2), 2005.

Praeger, R. L., *The Way that I Went*, 1937 (The Collins Press, 1999).

Robinson, Tim, *Connemara*, (*Part 1: Introduction and Gazetteer and Part 2: a one-inch map*), Folding Landscapes, 1990.

Whilde, Tony and Simms, Patrick, *West and North* (*New Irish Walking Guides*), Joss Lynam (ed.), Gill & Macmillan, 1991.

Whilde, Tony, *West* (*Irish Walks Guides/2*), Joss Lynam (ed.), Gill & Macmillan, 1978.

Glossary

Crag	A steep or rugged mass of rock – like a small cliff – that may stick out (or up) from the side of a mountain.
Crest	The top of a mountain or ridge or spur, often elongated.
Crannóg	A lake island dwelling mostly from the fifth to twelfth centuries.
Contouring	Walking along a slope while maintaining a given elevation, altitude or height.
Conglomerate	A sedimentary rock that is composed of various other rounded rocks and held together in a 'cemented' solid mass, found in some parts of Connemara and Mayo.
Fjord	A long, narrow sea valley with steep sides, created by a glacier.
Knoll	A small low hill or mound often surrounded by larger hills or mountains.
Machair	A rare fertile low-lying grassy plain on exposed coast adjacent to sand dunes with a high shell and peat-bog content, supporting rare flowers and birds.
Marram grass	A special type of long grass that grows on coastal sand dunes, which can tolerate salt and thrives under conditions of shifting sands and high winds.
Outcrop	A visible exposure of rock on the surface.
Ordovician	The geologic period between the Cambrian and Silurian periods that lasted from 488 million to 444 million years ago.
Precambrian	The geological period from the formation of the Earth (around 4.5 billion years ago) to the beginning of the Cambrian period (around 540 million years ago) when the first life forms appeared.
Quartzite	A hard crystalline metamorphic rock (normally sparkling white or grey), which was originally sandstone and is weather resistant and found on many ridges and hilltops in the Twelve Bens and the Maumturks.

Ridge	An exposed part of a hill or series of hills that forms a continuous elevated crest/top for some distance.
Saddle	A gap or mountain pass or low point between two hills (also coll).
Scrambling	A method of climbing rocky faces and ridges that requires the use of hands to hold body weight rather than just for balance; somewhere between hill walking and rock climbing.
Scree	Small loose stones, from Old Norse 'skritha'.
Silurian	A geologic period from about 416–440 million years ago and associated with specific flora and fauna.
Spot height	A black spot on a map marked with an altitude, normally representing a knoll, hill or mountain top and its associated height.
Spur	A lateral ridge or line of elevation projecting from the main body of a hill, mountain or mountain range, normally leading to a subsidiary summit of a mountain, lower than its parent summit and closely connected to it on the same ridgeline.
Tectonic	A geological process in which plates in the Earth's crust move in relation to one another.
Trig point	A triangular point on a map corresponding to a pillar on a mountain top, which was used to survey Ireland.